A Parrot in the Pepper Tree

a sort of sequel to

Driving Over Lemons

ANNIVERSARY EDITION
WITH AUTHOR INTERVIEW

D0280037

Sort Of
BOOKS

Published in June 2002 by SORT OF BOOKS,
PO Box 18678, London NW3 2FL
www.sortof.co.uk

8

Distributed by the Profile/Independent Alliance and TBS in all territories excluding the
United States and Canada.

Typeset in Iowan Old Style BT , THE Sans and Vitrina to a design by Henry Iles.
Printed and bound by CPI Group (UK) Ltd, Croydon, CR0 4YY
on Forest Stewardship Council (mixed sources) certified paper.

272pp
A catalogue record for this book is available from the British Library.
ISBN 978-0-9560038-1-2

A Parrot in the Pepper Tree

Chris Stewart

Acknowledgments

This book owes much to many people. I'd like to thank our valley neighbours and farm friends, Matias and Ants, Bernardo and Els, Cathy and John, Manolo, Trev, Joan and Patrick; Fernando and Jesus of *Nevadensis* for the beautiful gentian photo; Staffan Svensson for Swedish prompts and elk sign photos; Pilar Vazquez for Spanish prompts; Carole and Fiona, for more photos, and typing, and being my sisters; and above all, for their forebearance and leading roles in these pages, my heartfelt *abrazos* to Ana and Chloë.

Once again, my publishers Sort Of Books have been at the heart of this book and I thank Mark Ellingham and most particularly Natania Jansz, who has nursed and edited the manuscript from its earliest scribblings.

Sort Of and Chris thank: Peter Dyer for his inspired cover design and work beyond call of duty; Gig Binder for the perfectly timed photo shoots; Henry Iles for all the design within these pages; Gabi Pape for the author photo; Anne Hegerty for proofreading.

The events, places and people in this book are all real but to protect the innocent, and others, I have changed a few names and details.

For some great views of the Alpujarras, see *www.nevadensis.com*, maintained by this valuable mountain centre in Pampaneira. And if you would like to know more of Trev's art and design, you can view his work online at *www.wavesculptor.com*

Contents

DRIVING OVER ICE   1

LEMONS GALORE   21

MANOLO DEL MOLINILLO   39

WAITING FOR JUAN   55

TELEPHONY   70

LEAF OF THE MALE   86

FROM GENESIS TO THE BIG TOP   92

SPANISH GUITAR   107

LITERARY LIFE   121

A PARROT IN THE PEPPER TREE   133

ETHICS AND ANTI-CLERICALISM   146

BACK TO SCHOOL   165

WWOOFERS   175

AN ECO FOLLY   186

THE MEN IN TWEEDS   198

DEFENDERS OF THE RIVER   208

COMFORT AND JOY   218

A NIGHT UP THE MOUNTAIN   228

POND LIFE   238

AUTHOR INTERVIEW   249

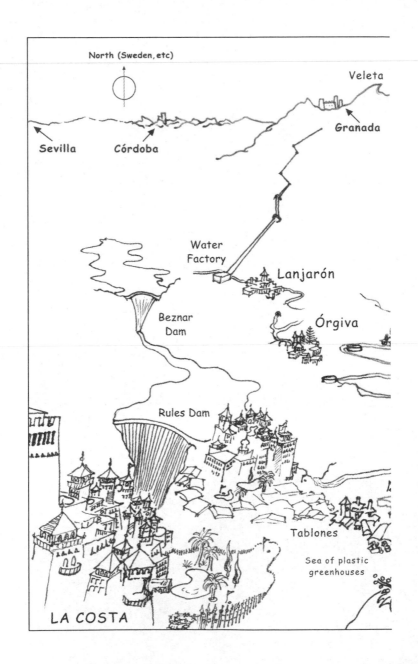

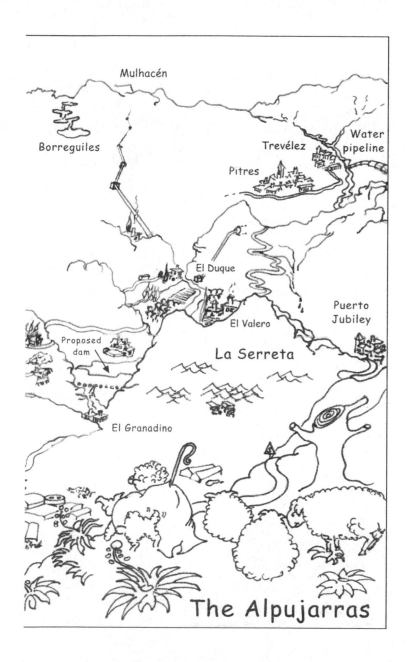

Mulhacén

Borreguiles

Trevélez

Water pipeline

Pitres

El Duque

El Valero

Puerto Jubiley

Proposed dam

La Serreta

El Granadino

The Alpujarras

DRIVING OVER ICE

I T WAS LATE AT NIGHT and for six long hours I had been driving along an icy tunnel of road into the snowy forest of northern Sweden. I hunched stiffly over the steering wheel to peer along a dismal beam at the monotony of pine trees and snow. One of my headlights had already given up the ghost, snuffed out in a futile struggle against the lashing ice and minus twenty-five degrees cold, and beyond the feeble pallor of its mate and the dim green glow of my dashboard there spread an endless blackness. For more than an hour, now, not a single car had passed me, and not a single lamplight glimmered through the trees. Country Swedes have an appealing tradition of leaving a light burning all night in the window to cheer the passing traveller, but for miles there had been nothing but the deep black of the star-studded sky, and the withering cold. Cocooned in the fuggy warmth of my hired Volvo I had the feeling of being further away from my fellow man than I had ever thought possible.

The radio was little help. The only station I had managed to pick up seemed entirely devoted to accordion and fiddle dances, the sort of low-key jolly fare you might expect at the funeral of a popular dog. I found it a little depressing. Instead, to keep awake, I fell into practising Mandarin Chinese, which for years I had been trying to learn. Counting out loud to yourself, *yi, er, san, si, wu,* is a good way of getting the hang of the tones and it helped me to forget how incredibly lonely I felt. Every time I got to a hundred or so, I would allow my mind to skip back to my home in Spain – the sun on a terrace of orange and lemon trees, Ana, my wife, and I lying on the grass, squinting up through the leaves, while our daughter Chloë hurled sticks for the dog – and then homesickness would strike with an almost physical stab and I'd start again – *yi, er, san, si, wu...*

As I worked my way up into the mid-sixties for a third time, the car engine began to play up. Every few minutes its steady rumble would be racked by an alarming series of coughs and judders, and the car would begin to vibrate, rising to a climax of lunatic shuddering. Then it would calm down again and resume its usual rumble.

Each time this happened I was beset by a vivid image of death by freezing. With the air outside at minus twenty-five degrees it wouldn't take long. The warmth of the cabin would dissipate in about ten minutes. That would allow me just enough time to grab all the clothes from my bag and put the whole lot on, capped by the enormous canvas and sheepskin coat (twenty quid in the Swedish Army Surplus), big mittens and woolly hat. My body heat would warm up the ensemble from the inside for about half an hour, then, via the usual process of thermodynamic exchange, the immense body of cold air would invade the tiny body of warmth that was me and overwhelm it. Jumping up and down, running on the spot, all that sort of stuff would prolong the sparks of warmth for a little longer, but I had read somewhere that you shouldn't do too much of it. Just how much was too much, though, I couldn't quite recall.

Still, as the engine revived once again and the car hummed on, I patted the dashboard affectionately in the hope that this would encourage it to shake off its troubles and drive me all the way to Norrskog, the farming village that I was heading for, still hours away through the forest.

I had picked the car up the evening before from Weekie's Car Lot, just outside the Copenhagen boat dock. Weekie had looked at me through his thick glasses and a fog of cigarette smoke. 'Take whichever one you want...,' he said, '...from over there,' and he pointed with a dismissive gesture to what looked like a scrap yard outside. I stepped out into the bone-chilling cold, the wind whipping across the Öresund shore, and inspected the offerings. There were old wrecks lying morosely here and there, some slumped down over a flat tyre, others with the bonnets off, revealing engines caked with grease and oil and a light covering of snow. This was where cars belonging to respectable, well-to-do folk came to rest, relegated to a twilight spot as transport for those who couldn't afford a proper hire car. But there was something appealing about Weekie's. It was like a sanctuary for old unloved horses; for a minimal fee you could take them out for a ride. I chose a pond-green Volvo, paid the small deposit, slung my kit in the back and headed off along the long long roads to northern Sweden.

I was here for a month to make money shearing sheep in the gloom of winter – a job that made enough to keep our small family and farm in Andalucia going for the rest of the year. It seemed that I was doomed to this annual purgatory. Our Spanish mountain farm was a cheap place to live and, with its produce to sustain us, we had few bills or outgoings. But we made hardly any money. There never seemed quite enough to cover the various domestic crises that beset us, like the generator and gas fridge packing up, or a wild boar trashing our new wire fence, or one of Chloë's beloved flamenco shoes getting ripped to shreds by the dogs. So these Swedish trips were essential.

As I drove on towards Norrskog, I mused, as I had each year before, on alternative ways of making ready cash. I had one new possibility this year, having sent off a few stories I'd written about life on our farm to some publishing friends in London. I wondered what they were making of my handwritten pages – too much about sheep and dogs probably – and allowed myself to daydream (if that's the right word in a pitch black Swedish afternoon) about a book contract and cheque. Meanwhile I kept a bleary eye open for elk.

Elk are the big danger on Swedish roads. You can't insure against them because the forests are literally swarming with the creatures. They leap out from the trees straight in front of your car – just a couple of seconds' warning and there they are. If you're unlucky, you knock the legs out from under them – a big elk is like a giant horse with antlers – and they come hurtling across the bonnet, through the windscreen and into the cabin with you. This intimacy is invariably fatal on both sides. For the elk, because it's been hit by a ton of speeding ironwork, and for you because you're pinned to your seat by your belt with an elk thrashing out its death throes in your lap. If you've really got your foot down, they can take the whole top of the car off, along with the top of the occupants. The Swedes do all they can to mitigate this unpleasantness, erecting tall fences along motorways and elk flashers to pick up the lights of cars and flash their warnings into the forest. But there are still hundreds of accidents every year.

I have an elk-avoidance trick that has long stood me in good stead. You find a big truck that's going about the same speed as you and you hang upon its tail. Of course you are constantly sprayed by all the muck kicked up by its back wheels, and if the trucker brakes hard and you happen not to notice, then you've all the inconvenience of a massive truck bursting through your windscreen instead of an elk. Still, on balance it's more restful than the strain of constantly scanning the dark band between forest and road for any signs of movement.

It was the prospect of an elk encounter that had led me to choose Weekie's Volvo. Piqued by Japanese competition in the car market, Volvo once ran an advert on billboards throughout Sweden. It showed a Japanese car full of very surprised Japanese and, standing before them, looming over the car, a vast bull elk. The text read 'Buy Volvo – there are no elk in Japan.'

The first town to break the endless vista of forest and dark was Norrköping (pronounced Gnaw-sherping). I stopped there to eat a dish of microwaved meatballs and to phone the first farm on my itinerary. This occupied a small island three hundred miles to the north.

'The sea is frozen over,' the farmer told me on the phone. 'You can drive across to us if you don't come too close in to the shore. The ice is a bit thin by the reeds. I'll hang a red bucket in the birch tree by the track, so you'll know where to turn off.'

'Of course,' I said, not really absorbing the information.

As I urged the old car on out into the huge darkness beyond the streetlights of the town, the night folded over me like the sea. The heater whirred away to itself, filling the cabin with a warm fug, and for a couple of hours the engine ran smoothly. I was lulled and warm and tired. Then, just as I was wriggling around to get myself comfortable in the seat, the engine cut out. It juddered, then fired and started again, then coughed and stopped. My blood turned cold and my arms and legs went weak.

I got out. Snow was falling now, fast and thick, damping down the already heavy silence. It was so perfectly quiet I could hear my blood squeezing through the capillaries. I heard my heart thumping rhythmically and sensed the infinitesimal humming of neurons in my brain.

The car ticked and creaked as the hot metal cooled. I stood there for perhaps a minute, hardly breathing for fear of breaking the extraordinary spell of silence. Then the cold was too much for me and I climbed back in. If I left the car to cool for a few minutes, it might start again. I sat behind the wheel with my mouth open, watching the heavy flakes falling in the pale glow of the snow. In minutes the car was cold, all the warmth in the cabin was gone. I tried the starter. The engine fired. I switched the headlight on and moved off unsteadily along the road.

The car was running very roughly now, not helped by a fresh snowstorm. Snowstorms can have a dangerously hypnotic effect, as the snow seems to form a whirling tunnel in front of you and it can be difficult to take your eyes from it. I was starting to get really worried. My map showed a small town about twenty kilometres on, so I kept going, heart in mouth, focused on the point where all my problems would end.

The town was called Åbro and as I rolled in, at eleven o'clock, it looked like it had been tucked up in bed for hours. A lone pizza place was shuttered and the only light came from the streetlights. But as I chugged on around the backstreets I came upon a dimly lit sign that said 'Hotel'.

I parked the car and rang the bell. I waited and shivered a bit and gasped at the sheer weight of the falling snow. The Volvo creaked beside me. I rang the bell again. Still nothing, not a light, not a sound. At last an upstairs window opened.

'Yes? What do you want?' came the curt voice of a middle-aged woman.

'Ah, um – this is the hotel is it?'

'Yes'

'Well, my car has broken down and I'd be really grateful if you could let me have a bed for the night.'

'You can't, we have no *övernattning*.'

'What do you mean you have no *övernattning*?'

'I mean we have no *övernattning*!'

'This isn't a hotel then?'

'Yes, it is a hotel.'

'Well if it is a hotel then surely I can stay the night.'

'It is a hotel but you can't stay the night because we have no *övernattning*,' she repeated firmly, and, as if this brought things to a satisfactory conclusion, slammed the window shut. I shouted that as I had nowhere else to sleep it would be entirely her responsibility if I froze to death. However, I might as well have yelled at the snow. This hotelier was not going to relent for one feeble foreigner with a grudge about its policy on *övernattning* – which, incidentally, means staying the night.

Half an hour earlier, I would have said that I had reached rock bottom but it was nothing to this new despair. My options for getting through that bitter night were looking extremely grim. I decided to sleep on the back seat of the car outside the wretched hotel and leave the engine running, both for warmth and to annoy the harpie of the hotel. There was a risk that I'd asphyxiate or freeze, but at least I'd have the satisfaction of leaving an untidy heap – car and frozen body – on the hotel's doorstep in the morning.

I lay down, fully clothed and with a few extra layers added for good measure, beneath the sheepskin coat. My heart was full of spleen, my head full of wrath, and my teeth chattered. Soon, though, I slept and when I awoke in the early morning hours, the motor was still purring and the heater humming away and I was alive. I breathed in, exultantly, and felt the hairs in my nostrils shrivel and freeze – it's very cold indeed when they do that.

I left that town still fulminating about the hotel. What could be the use of such a ludicrous thing? What nefarious purpose could it possibly serve? It seemed most unlikely that the town's upstanding inhabitants were whooping it up in rooms rented hourly. Swedish country towns are not known for their erotic shenanigans, so it had to be for drinking: there is nowhere in rural Sweden where you can sit down in congenial surroundings and order a pint of beer, or work your way reflectively through a bottle of wine. The preferred method is to swig from a bottle of vodka or cheap whisky discreetly hidden in a brown paper bag. The hotel would be a drinking club, that's what.

Within an hour, however, my anger had vanished before the mechanical ministrations of Matts, a thick-set, bristly man with kindly eyes, who helped me push the car to his workshop on the edge of the next village. Matts knew exactly what was wrong and, while his wife brought me steaming cups of tea, he beavered around with screwdriver and wrench, and in half an hour declared it fixed. I asked him how much I owed, a little nervous as repairs of any sort are astronomical in Sweden.

'Oh, don't worry about it,' he insisted. 'I used to be on the road myself when I was young, and anyway it's a pleasure to help out a traveller from abroad; we don't get many here.' I pressed him but he refused and he waved me a cheery good-bye as the car and I purred off into the woods. Matts was the sort of Swede who could make *övernattning* in a refrigerated van seem bearable.

Pleased with this turn of events, I began to enjoy the Swedish landscape. The clouds had lifted and the sun crawled low into the frozen blue sky. The snow glittered on the trees and as the countryside opened out a little I saw the perfect white of the frozen sea beneath a fresh fall of snow. Spotting the red bucket in a silver birch, I wound down a sinuous track through the woods, pure white and dappled with sunlight. At the bottom of the track was a little boat dock deep in snow, and sure enough, just beside it the track dipped down the bank and headed out to sea. A couple of miles off I could see some pine-covered islands dark against the dazzling white sea. The tyres of the car squeaked on the new snow as I eased gingerly down the bank onto the marked road. Then, wincing at every bump or crunch, I set off to drive across the sea.

'What happens if I fall through the ice?' I thought to myself. The car would sink like a brick in the icy water, of course. Then, assuming I did manage to squeeze out and swim up to the hole made by the car (no easy matter), I'd still have to scrabble out onto the thick walls of ice. I remembered that you can't do this without ice spikes. You need one in each hand to get enough grip on the ice to be able to haul yourself out. And, even if you happen to have a pair handy and the strength to do the hauling, how long would you last, sopping wet and sitting on a sea of ice?

As I moved cautiously forward, following the marker buoys and thinking these dark thoughts, I saw a small yellow object, like a toy van, leave the island and turn my way. It grew quickly, reaching enormous proportions as it hurtled past in a flurry of snow. The driver, fag hanging out of his mouth, gave me a jolly grin. It was a furniture lorry. I felt relieved and then a little worried that its huge weight might have cracked the solid ice.

'How do those people know the day the ice is no longer safe to drive a furniture lorry across?' I wondered. But luck was with me and soon I arrived at the yellow reeds around the island. I stopped the car and stepped gingerly out onto the ice. Looking back I saw the lorry vanishing in the brightness.

When I switched off the engine, I was again struck by the extraordinary stillness of the Swedish winter. There is no wind, and even if there were, the trees would be too heavy with their thick load of frozen snow to move. There are no birds to sing and the sea is silenced by its sarcophagus of ice. The only sound in the landscape is you.

These thoughts were cut short by the sudden clatter of a snow scooter. A farmer, clad in an orange boilersuit and woolly hat, appeared through a gap in the trees, dismounted and trudged towards my car. '*Hej!*' he offered sadly. 'Welcome to Norbo.' He took some time in getting his right mitten off while he gazed blankly at the snow. Then he held out a pale pink and white hand. 'Björn,' he muttered, withdrawing the proffered hand quickly from my grip.

'Chris,' said I.

'Welcome to Norbo,' he said again.

'*Tak* – thanks,' I replied, trying to keep the conversation rolling, though it seemed to have a finality about it.

Björn was aged about thirty, a pink, rounded man with a melancholy look about him. He seemed more comfortable with silence than small talk although he did allow a wan smile to flicker across his muted features when our eyes met. I gave him a big grin but this seemed a little too much for him and he looked away, affecting a quiet cough into his mittens.

In amicable silence we loaded my clobber onto the trailer that dragged behind the scooter, mounted up, and scudded over the ice to the shore. Half hidden by the pines was a big yellow house, part stone and part timber. It had recently had a coat of paint but needed a bit of fundamental attention to its carpentry to bring it in line with the usual immaculate turnout of Swedish houses. But as the Swedes themselves so nicely put it: *Bättre lite skit i hörnet än ett rent helvete* – 'Better a little shit in the corner than a clean hell.'

We passed the farmhouse and weaved our way through a birch wood to the sheep's quarters. This was a cathedral of timber, a colossal hulk of faded red planks and rotting beams. From inside came the baaing of hundreds of sheep, like the buzzing of a swarm of huge bees.

Björn took a shovel and with a few deft strokes in the snow revealed a little wooden door. With his knife he cut the string that secured it, and kicked it hard. It graunched inwards, enough for us to squeeze through. As we entered, the baaing became deafening, and my nose was assailed by the thick miasma of damp wool, mouldy hay and sheepshit.

Gradually my eyes adapted to the gloom – what little light there was entered through cracks in the planking and dusty windows – and to a truly disheartening sight. There were sheep everywhere, grubby black creatures with steam rising from their backs. The steam hung in a great smelly cloud and within the cloud, seemingly drifting in the air, were even more sheep. They were wandering along plankways that led into the cavernous vault of the barn. Everywhere were huge malodorous bales of hay and silage, with sheep on them and in them, like weevils in a biscuit.

'Bit of a balls-up, eh Björn?' I muttered in a feeble understatement. I was looking at one of the grimmest jobs I'd had to do in ten years of work in Sweden.

Björn looked crestfallen. His eyelashes brushed his cheeks as he looked down and wrung his hands a little.

'You see, it's been a terrible year,' he said quietly.

'It certainly has, Björn – these sheep look like shit! Still, don't you worry about it, we'll get at them this afternoon and in a couple of days they'll look like new!'

'Well then, shall we go and have something to eat?' he said, with the beginnings of a grin. I decided that I liked Björn.

Björn's parents, Tord and Mia, were waiting for us in the kitchen. Unlike the barn this had a scrubbed, colourful look – it was clearly Mia's domain – and a warm smell of cinnamon buns and coffee wafted towards us from a tray on the broad wooden table.

'Come and eat,' intoned Mia, clumping back to the oven and then bending at the hip in a stiff bow to lift out another tray of buns. She winced a little before straightening up.

'We hope you'll stay,' she added and glanced at her husband as if calling on him to flesh out the invite. Tord, a larger, rounder, pinker version of Björn, smiled broadly at me but seemed unwilling to commit himself to words. Instead he helped himself to another bun, and gestured that I should do the same.

'Thank you, these are nice buns,' I enthused. It was true they were nice buns, with lots of cinnamon and sugar, but they were also the same as every other bun I'd tasted from the north to the south of rural Sweden on any given day.

'*Aah det är de* – that they are...' Tord agreed, and gestured towards the coffee pot.

'Nice coffee,' I commented, a mite less sincerely as I hate coffee that's been boiled twice. This didn't, however, seem the moment for experimental chit-chat.

I looked meaningfully at Björn. He nodded and we rose from the table to go back to the sheep shed. Back in the barn I changed into icy, grease-caked shearing clothes and hung my machine in a corner while Björn set up a mercury lamp. It was only half past two but the sun was dropping fast. The shabby black sheep surrounded us, munching insolently, and as the mercury lamp built up to full power I was illuminated in a pool of bluish white light like an actor in a very fringe theatre. Björn disappeared into the darkness and came back with a sheep. The first customer of the day. I pulled the starter cord.

The first stroke when you shear a sheep goes down across the brisket and out over the belly – or it should do. But the machine stuck almost immediately on a matted snag of belly-wool. I pushed a little harder, took the comb out and tried another angle. Same thing. I pushed and pulled and tugged and strained but still that first bit of wool of the day refused to come off. Either Björn had selected the worst sheep in the flock for me or else I was in for a time of utmost misery.

The sheep was bad all over but eventually I managed to get most of its wool off, by dint of merciless pushing and jabbing and pulling the more reluctant bits off with my hand. She looked awful as she tripped back into the darkness.

'I'm sorry about that, Björn,' I gasped. 'She looks a fright, but it's taken nearly fifteen minutes to do one bloody sheep. If there are as many as you say there are then we're going to be here all week, and it's going to be a god-awful week!'

Björn looked miserable. 'Maybe this one is a little better,' he offered hopefully, dragging the next sheep from the shadows.

But it wasn't. Nor was the next one. Then came one that you could describe only with expletives. I straightened up and groaned with the pain in my back. I had been at it for an hour and I had done four sheep. There were supposed to be three hundred-odd sheep in the flock... that would be seventy-five hours of this misery.

With a groan I looked ahead through the long tunnel of the week – the cold, the smelly barn – and most of all the loneliness, for much as I liked Björn, neither he nor his parents were the sort of folks you'd want to spend a whole week with. I started thinking about doing a bunk there and then.

'Who normally shears these sheep, Björn?'

'I usually do it myself, only I've hurt my back – chainsawing in the woods.' The old Swedish complaint.

Björn seemed to be reading my thoughts – and he looked desperate. With good reason. If I didn't shear these sheep, then I couldn't see anybody else coming all the way to do it. I thought about the long drive up here, the money that I needed, the worsening task I'd be leaving behind, and relented. I signalled to Björn to pull out another sheep.

Now I don't want to go on too much about sheep-shearing, but four sheep an hour is hell. With average clean good sheep I could normally manage twenty to twenty-five sheep an hour. Going at that rate the body is in constant fluid movement, all the muscles well exercised and freely moving in what amounts to almost a choreographed dance. But when you're bent over the same sheep, poking, jabbing and heaving in the same horrible posture, then the pain in the lower back, the middle back and the legs is almost unbearable – and it's no ball for the sheep, either.

Björn stood miserably beside me, his breath steaming in the dank air of the barn, while I heaved and struggled with the sheep. As the day progressed, my thoughts turned black and I silently cursed everybody and everything: Björn and his wretched sheep and his disgusting barn and his parents. I was nothing but bitterness and back-pain. What a way to earn a living! What a waste of life!

'Let's finish now,' urged Björn, seeing the demons take hold.

'No, let's do two more. That way there'll be two less at the end of the job.'

Björn brought two more sheep and as if I were being rewarded for steadfastness of character they were both fliers. Young and firm-fleshed and well rounded they sat meek and compliant on the board as the wool peeled away like grey silk.

I staggered and stretched and thought about beer. Then I remembered that I was in rural Sweden. A light beer, brewed by some vile industrial chemical process, would be the best I could hope for. It might even be *lättöl* – alcohol 'free' and lacking also any flavour, aroma or pleasure. It always makes me think of George Orwell's 'Victory Beer' in *1984*.

I hung up the shears and together Björn and I trudged across the frozen yard, the snow squeaking beneath our boots – which means, if I've got it right, that it's ten degrees or more below zero. Björn wrenched open the farmhouse door and we crowded in among ranks of evil-smelling boots and farm-wear. We peeled off our outer layers and padded in flopping woollen socks into the bright kitchen. Tord was there, smiling broadly as usual. He passed me a bottle of *lättöl* and a pink-tinged plastic beaker.

'Thanks shall you have,' I said in that curious Swedish way.

Tord watched as I worked my way without enthusiasm through the beer. Tonight, he said, we would be going to the Norrskog Farmers' Study Circle weekly meeting. It would be most interesting for me, he thought, to come along and take part in the proceedings. I thought about declining. It certainly wouldn't be a wild evening out, but then I pictured us all sitting through that first night staring at a diminishing pile of cinnamon buns and sipping *lättöl* round the kitchen table. I went to get my coat.

We whizzed along icy roads in Tord's car towards a village hall in a clearing in the woods, stopping on the way to pick up Ernst, the chairman of the study circle, who lived in a little red house by the roadside. Ernst was small and wiry with a thin, slightly lop-sided mouth, and Tord seemed very much in awe of him. At the hall, Tord ushered me through the decompression chamber, a set of heavy double doors, and into the warm, brightly-lit wooden room. Motley groups of tall thick-set men in woollen shirts and baseball caps milled uncertainly about, sipping fruit squash from paper cups. These men worked alone deep in the woods with their chainsaws, or communed with their pigs in dark barns with the snow stacked up high against the windows. Small talk was not what they were good at and a grateful silence fell on the spasmodic and constipated attempts at conversation as Tord and Ernst entered.

'*Hejsan!*' (hello there) called Ernst as we passed through the hall. Everyone looked down at their boots and shuffled in acute embarrassment. '*Hej*, Ernst!' muttered some brave soul. '*Hej, hej, hej...*' came the quiet chorus. It was clear that Ernst ran the show, such as it was, and when he spoke people listened, and whatever he said was greeted with relief because it meant that nobody else would be obliged to say anything. Thus the assembled company hung upon his lips.

'Tonight we have an Englishman with us,' announced Ernst. 'He is going to tell us about farming in England.'

'Bloody hell, Ernst, I can't...' I spluttered, before my words were stifled in a bout of muted clapping. I looked down at the sea of upturned baseball caps – well, there were twenty of them at least – and began.

'Er, good evening...' I said.

'*Go'afton,*' replied one or two.

There was a pause.

'I am really no expert,' I hazarded, playing for time. 'I don't know much about the technical side of farming or even the ordinary stuff like dry matter conversion rates and subsidy clawback... perhaps I could, er, just answer a few of your questions about animals and crops?'

The baseball caps were trained expectantly upon me but nobody chose to break the silence, until at last Ernst set the ball rolling. 'Kris,' he began (*kris* – pronounced *krees* – means crisis in Swedish). 'Tell us, how big do you sell a cow in England?'

I saw from a concerted nodding of the hats that this was a subject that excited universal interest. But I hadn't the first idea how big we sold a cow in England. I tried to visualise a cow – the sort of fat cow that might be for sale. They're huge, cows are, with great pendulous bellies and massive heads. I did a quick mental calculation.

'Well, I suppose about a couple of tons.'

A gasp came from the hats, followed by animated mumbling. I had clearly erred on the high side here.

'Of course,' I added. 'That would be a good big one – really, a hell of a big one. A more normal one would be around the one-and-a-half ton mark, I suppose.'

More incredulous gasping. I was in deep.

'And of course a lot of them are quite a bit smaller... some of them would probably go as low as a ton – the runts, that is.'

It got worse as the session wore on. By the end of the evening I seemed to have recreated England as a land populated by creatures of mythical proportions and bursting with the most improbable crops and astonishing yields.

In the car, afterwards, Björn broke the thick silence. 'Don't worry, Kris,' he said. 'People put too much emphasis on facts.'

There was a pause.

'What you said was... well, unusual. It woke people up.'

'Björn,' I groaned. 'How could I have said that a cow weighed two tons? That's nearly three times the normal size! They must think I'm an absolute and utter dickhead.'

'I don't know,' said Tord, from the back. His voice was on the verge of hysteria. 'It's not as if you offered to muck them out!'

I grew quite fond of Björn during the week at Norbo. Our glum days together in the sheep shed had become almost companionable, and on a couple of nights we went skiing in the moonlight across the sea, and on another to a local dance where we leaned against a wall in the shadows watching the girls and swigging whisky from a Coca-Cola bottle hidden in a brown paper bag.

When Björn announced, 'There's only four left, I think,' I felt a surge of affection for my melancholy friend, which endured even as the four sheep turned into fifteen or more hidden in the shadows. As we made for the door of the barn, the sun came out and shone in needle-fine shafts through the holes in the rotten cladding of the walls, illuminating bits of shorn sheep, flanks heaving, breath steaming. Björn surveyed his flock with evident relief and, removing his mitten, shook my hand formally. 'Thanks shall you have,' he said.

The next morning, I slung my kit in the car and headed back across the sea, moving around to another half dozen farms separated by wearying drives through elk-infested forest.

As usual, the trip lasted about a month – a long time away from home, and a lot of time to spend in the dark, on the road or with sheep. The high point was when a letter from home caught up with me at one of the farms. Chloë had written me a little poem, in Spanish and accompanied by a picture of a princess, and Ana had written a wonderful and witty letter, which carried momentous news.

Apparently my publishing friends in London reckoned they might be able to make something of my stories about the farm, and they had sent an advance so that I could get my head down and finish it. 'Prepare yourself for being a bestselling author,' noted Ana wryly. 'All you have to do is sell a few lorryloads of books and you need never go shearing in Sweden again.'

I grinned bovinely at this remote prospect, much as a giant cow might grin in the meadows of England.

LEMONS GALORE

I CLIMBED OFF THE BUS IN ORGIVA, the small provincial town and hub of urban life in the Western Alpujarras, and squinted into the bright April sunshine. After a month away, even the dump of a bus stop seemed gay and lively, flanked as it was by the pastel-green optician's and the red and white supermarket, with some colourful plastic bags blowing in the wind round the wheelie-bins. I breathed in deep the inimitable Spanish town smell of coffee, garlic and black tobacco, and, shouldering my pack, set off for home. I always prefer to do the last bit of the journey home on foot; it adds a frisson of romance and gives me an opportunity to enjoy the sights and sounds of the countryside on the way. It takes about an hour and a half, in the unlikely event that you don't find someone to stop and talk to.

Crossing the dribble of the Río Seco, I strode down into the *vega* – the fields of olives, oranges and vegetables that surround the town – and out along the road towards Tíjolas (sounds like 'tickle us'). The roadside, which wound in and out of the river gullies and up and down the hills, was cushioned with tender new grass and clumps of dazzling yellow oxalis. The dark foliage of the orange and lemon trees was hung with bright fruit – a few here and there rolling across the road. As the first of the houses appeared, the village dogs that lay slumped on the warm road, roused themselves to bark at me.

'Adiós,' called the village women peering from behind the clouds of geraniums and margaritas that burst from old paint tins on their patios. 'Adiós,' I replied, raising my arm in greeting. 'Goodbye, Goodbye.' This is the standard greeting to someone passing by. It may seem a little odd to call 'adiós' to someone approaching, but if you don't stop there is a certain logic in it.

Leaving Tíjolas behind me, I struck up the track that climbs through rocks and scrub to the ridge at the edge of our valley. At the top I unslung my pack and sat down on a warm rock to gaze back over the *vega*. A patchwork of neat fields, of all different colours and textures, stretched away below me. A blue plume of smoke rose into the still air and silver ribbons of water weaved among the fields, glittering in the sunlight. I thought of the dark pine forests of Sweden labouring beneath their burden of ice, and allowed myself a broad, self-satisfied grin. Then I hoisted my pack again and set off up the last part of the hill.

The roaring of the river, tumbling out through the gorge far below the road, was the only sound apart from the trudging of my feet in the dust. A few more minutes tramping, and I reached the gap in the rock which is the first point from which you can see El Valero, our home – tiny and distant on the far side of the river. A huge eucalyptus tree hides the house from the road but I could see the river fields with their crop of alfalfa, and the brighter greens of the watered terraces below the *acequia* (one of the Moorish irrigation channels that carries water along the hillside from the river to the farm). Higher up, I picked out the sheep moving through the scrub, while nearby, Lola, my horse, stood tethered in the riverbed, flicking away at the flies.

'Nearly home,' I thought to myself as I walked on round the bend in the track to the dead almond tree – the spot where visitors announce their arrival, either by sounding the horn or by whooping. Cupping my hands together, I whooped. It's not a loud noise but over the years Ana and I have perfected just the right pitch so that either of us can hear the other from even the most distant corners of the valley. Even if we don't hear the whoop, it never fails to set the dogs barking, and sure enough, I heard the yapping of Big, our terrier, the deep bass woofing of our sheepdog, Bumble, and a sonorous quack from Bonka, her mother. It's hard to say why a dog should quack like a duck, but she always has done and I'd be sorry if she were ever to change.

I caught sight of a slim figure waving down by the mandarin terrace. It was Ana. Screwing up my eyes I tried to fix the details – she'd had a haircut, no it was a hat – but I was too far off to make it out. Then there was a frantic rustling of a tree and all of a sudden a little figure with a mop of curly blonde hair appeared from under a branch, waving excitedly: Chloë, my five-year-old daughter. I whooped some more, and hollered, and jumped up and down waving frantically, and then strode on into the valley. It's odd, being able to look down on your home some time before you get there – a sort of sneak preview. I still had a good twenty minutes to go.

I walked along the road, cut dramatically into the rock here above the river, for another kilometre, then slithered and slipped down the steep path that led to the *acequia*. Here the air was cooled by the racing water, as I made my way along the bank beneath the shade of the eucalyptus.

Finally I took the track that dropped down to the river-bed and started making my way upriver towards the bridge. On the shingle flat by the river I spotted a figure, a short, powerfully built man in a straw hat and torn shirt. He was crouching, half hidden in the scrub, seemingly absorbed by something on the ground. It was my neighbour, Domingo.

Domingo saw me as I spotted him and beckoned me over. He was bending pensively over a sick-looking sheep, poking her here and there. He pulled back an eyelid and peered in.

'It's the same old thing,' he said without looking up, 'eyes like potatoes. Look, there's no colour in them.'

Domingo has no talent at all for greetings.

The sheep lay there heaving and looking resigned in the way that sheep do. 'She looks a bit off colour,' I observed, thinking in fact that she was a goner.

'She is,' he replied, grinning up at me. 'I thought it might be the liver. I've noticed some cysts appearing on the liver of one or two of the sheep that have died recently. But they also had stomachs full of *albaida*, so it's hard to know what finished them off.' (*Albaida* is *Anthyllis cytisoides*, a yellow flowering shrub that covers the hills, and at this time of year is thick with flowers and seeds – a tasty, high-protein snack if nibbled in moderation but often fatal if gorged upon.)

'How the hell do you know that, Domingo?' I exclaimed. 'You need an autopsy to find out that sort of stuff.'

Domingo shrugged. 'Well, they're no good to anyone when they're dead, are they? You might as well open them up and have a look inside.' Then he slapped the sheep on the side and rolled her over onto her belly.

'She'll be okay though – she's not too far gone yet.'

He stood up and stretched, wiping the sweat from his brow with the back of his arm, and I watched as the sheep tottered drunkenly off to slump in the shade beneath a tamarisk tree. I'm not bad at diagnosing ovine ailments, but Domingo it seemed, was in the advanced class.

'So,' he said, smiling broadly and holding out a hand, 'How was Sweden?'

'It wasn't too bad,' I answered and, spurred on by his unusually expansive opening, I told him all about my contract to write a book. He listened quietly.

'Hmm, sounds good if you like that sort of thing,' he commented, and then started on about some dispute over grazing. I felt oddly disappointed by his lack of interest.

'And what about you, Domingo, how's things over your side of the river? And how's Antonia?'

'We're alright,' he answered. 'I've been doing some other things as well. Maybe you should come and have a look. Why don't you come...' – he looked down, poking a stone about with his sneaker – '...come to dinner, all of you, tomorrow night.'

And that was it, a simple invitation, rather awkwardly given. But I think we both recognised it as something different. Never in the thirteen years that I'd lived in the valley had Domingo invited me formally to a meal. It was obvious that each of our lives had tilted slightly on its axis. Here was I with a book deal and here was Domingo issuing dinner invitations.

I looked at him quizzically for a moment.

'Well... yes, of course we'll come,' I said.

We stood together for a little longer while Domingo expanded on the problems he was having with some hunters and landowners on the hill behind us. Then he untied his donkey from the bunch of reeds where she was tethered, mounted and trotted off up the track. I walked on towards the bridge lost in thought about Domingo and the quirk of fate that had paired him off with a sculptress from Holland.

For close on forty years, Domingo had led a quiet, rather lonely existence on his family farm. He seemed contented enough, but the life and the work barely tapped his keen intelligence and thirst for new ideas and knowledge. A brief spell working in a factory in Barcelona put paid to whatever wanderlust he might have had and instead he set about learning what he could of north European notions and ways from his foreign neighbours – Bernardo and Isabel, a Dutch couple who lived at La Cenicera just down the valley, and ourselves.

Then one summer a freckly, auburn-haired Dutchwoman called Antonia arrived. She was making scuptures of the various animals she encountered in our valley, and she stayed on, in a makeshift home in the abandoned farmhouse at La Herradura. Domingo's sheep occasionally grazed the Herradura, but the summer Antonia moved in they became a fixture, grazing the place till it looked like a billiard table. By the time the rains began in October, Domingo had persuaded Antonia to move in with him at his farm, and immediately set about rebuilding the house to accommodate his first and only love and her work.

Antonia returned to Holland for much of the winter, to drum up commissions and see to the casting in bronze of her models, but she came back to the valley in early spring. Ana had written to me that they had become inseparable, and were currently working together re-organising Domingo's shabby old *cortijo*. I was intrigued to see what was happening.

I crossed our rickety wooden bridge and reached the greenery of the river fields. At the top are the giant plumes of the eucalyptus wood, towering over the olives that ring the alfalfa field. The alfalfa itself is the deepest green you can imagine, and scattered with little blue flowers, the very sight of which cools you on a summer day. The track passes here through a virtual tunnel of huge bramble-bushes, tamarisks and broom, and then the hill up to the house starts.

This is the point where I always begin to worry about my homecoming. Will Ana and Chloë be as pleased to see me as I like to think they would, or will they be cool and a little resentful as I turn up and muscle back into their lives, just as they had got used to being without me? Will they be disappointed to find that after all these long weeks apart,

I'm still just the same ordinary bloke they knew before? As I trudged up the hill I started to brood on these thoughts, and then came the dogs, tearing down the hill wagging their tails in insane delight, jumping up and covering me with dust and slobber. They knew who I was, and didn't give a stuff that I was ordinary. I took heart.

Then with barely a moment for me to fling out my arms, Chloë came cannoning into my chest. I looked up from this melee of arms, legs and paws to see Ana smiling from the terrace. Chloë looked up at the same moment and we all grinned a little shyly at each other.

The next evening, with a bottle of wine tucked under one arm, and swinging Chloë along between us with the other, we ambled across the valley to Domingo and Antonia's farmhouse. From behind we could hear the distant howling of the dogs, who took a dim view of being tied up on the terrace. The air was a lot cooler down in the valley and a barely perceptible breeze brought us the heady scent of the flowering retama along with an occasional whiff of sheep dung.

Domingo's *tinao* – the small covered patio that constitutes the main living space of all Alpujarran houses – had a lot more herbage and greenery than I remembered, and the gloomy old kitchen now had a skylight, a recent innovation consisting of a hole bashed in the roof covered by the windscreen of the old Mercedes van that had lain for as long as I could remember in the bushes by his chicken shed. This had improved things to the extent that you could see what you were doing in the kitchen. Before, Domingo's mother had performed her kitchen duties more by feel and instinct.

We drew up our chairs to the table, in the middle of which stood a jam jar, with one of those pretty home bottling labels stuck across the front. I picked it up and idly turned it. The label, written in careful script, read *Quince and Walnut Marmalade*. 'It's good, but I think I put too much quince in that one,' said Domingo. 'Here, this one's better, you should take this one home with you,' and he handed me a new jar from the shelf. The label this time read *Loquat and Ginger*.

'Who did the labels?' I asked.

'I did,' said Domingo.

'Domingo has some funny ideas about jam,' commented Antonia, as if experimenting with jams was the most natural occupation for an Alpujarran shepherd. 'But sometimes they really do work. That one there is delicious.' Ana looked studiedly at me, and kicked me under the table to stop me gaping, while Antonia began serving us all some mysterious concoction that she had prepared. It was spicy with ginger and fresh coriander in it. As its oriental flavours burst within me, I reflected on the fact that something odd was happening in our small valley.

After eating, we went to look at the 'studio', which Domingo was in the process of converting from the room where they used to keep the pigs. Chloë and Ana wandered about admiring the bronzes – some of them were old friends, including a fine model of Lola, and a fearsome wild boar. Ana picked up a new one – a beautifully modelled ibex, and turned to show it to me, cradling it carefully in her hand.

'What do you think of it?' asked Antonia, grinning.

'It's wonderful,' we replied simultaneously. 'One of your very best, Antonia,' I added. 'It really captures the grace of an ibex.'

'The foundry workers thought so, too, and they don't usually comment on the stuff they cast,' she added. 'I'd be flattered if it was mine.' And she turned to smile at Domingo. 'He doesn't realise what a talent he has.'

Ana and I stared incredulously from the ibex to the sculptor. This was further extraordinary news and I struggled to take in its full import. Ana, as usual, was one step ahead.

'You mean you made it?' she exclaimed.

'Bah, it's nothing,' Domingo shrugged. 'I just watched it for a while and copied it.' Then, warming to the role of exhibiting artist, he fetched down the various bulls, ibex and horses that he had modelled in wax, using tools that he had made for himself out of wood and cane.

If Antonia felt at all uneasy about Domingo's emergence as a fellow sculptor, then she hid it well. I remembered how I had taught Domingo to shear sheep, and how the pupil had outstripped his master within a very short time.

'I thought I'd have a go selling some of them,' continued Domingo. 'Antonia thinks she can get some of my animals into a gallery on the coast. Maybe it's something I can do when my bones get too old for chasing sheep up and down these mountains all day.'

Back at El Valero, I decided the time had come to take my own new career by the horns. I got up uncharacteristically early and plunged myself into my morning tasks. I had been inspired by Domingo's example and today was the day I was going to sort myself out a study and become a writer.

First, Ana got her morning cup of tea rather earlier than she might have wished; then I fed the chickens, then the pigeons, then I went down to the stable to let the sheep out. Having done that, I took the path that skirts the house to a low building just below the ancient threshing floor and pushed open the wooden door. This was the *cámara* – the store-room – where Pedro Romero, the last owner of the farm, had kept his dry goods. When we first arrived, it had been festooned with strings of peppers, onions, garlic and yellowing hunks of *tocino* – pig fat. On the floor were piles of salt, heaps of maize husks, sacks of grain and, in the corner, an ancient iron machine with a flywheel and a handle for de-husking cobs.

The husking machine was still there in the corner, surrounded now by a different detritus: old flower-pots, boxes of clothes and superannuated toys and dusty books – and a guitar, waiting upon my whim, like a well-loved dog. This was going to be the place where I would sit and write my book.

I heaved the corn husking machine out of the way, blew the dust off the table and gave it a scrub with an old tee-shirt. Then I sat down, sharpened some pencils, filled my pen and fished about for the right sort of paper to get started on. With a flourish, I wrote the words *El Libro* at the top of the page.

I paused and looked at it for a moment with pleasure, then looked out of the window at the pigeons flying round the eucalyptus tree. At the foot of the eucalyptus tree is Ana's kitchen garden. I caught sight of a small movement in the corner by the strawberries... Hell and damnation! It was a sheep! The sheep were attacking the vegetable patch! Quick as a flash I hared out of the door and down the hill. This could have the makings of a grade A disaster. Ana would be furious, and the sheep, whose popularity with my womenfolk was already at a pretty low ebb, would run the risk of being expelled from the farm.

'What's happening?' shouted Ana as I flailed past the house.

'Nothing, I'm just going for a walk!' I yelled, disappearing in a cloud of dust and exuberantly barking dogs down the track.

'If those wretched sheep are on the vegetable patch again...' Ana began, but the threat was drowned out by the sound of me leaping over the fence and crashing through the salsola bushes.

Between the dogs and me, and with a good deal of yelling and barking, we managed to get the sheep out of the vegetables with only a little collateral damage. With foul oaths I drove them away and then set to patching up the holes they had come through.

So much for my first morning as a writer.

That first month back at home passed in a torment of delays and interruptions as I tried to take my first literary steps. There were farm jobs that had stacked up in my absence: the *acequias* needed clearing, the stable wanted mucking out, and there was a crop of alfalfa that needed scything. Chloë needed to be ferried to and from the school bus stop at the other end of the valley, and the fencing around Ana's vegetable patch needed mending properly, and the car needed taking to pieces – and then someone needed to be found to put it back together again. And so it went on and on and on until, as often happens, a breaking point was reached and I was forced to look for help.

The day I finally decided that things were getting out of hand, and that some sort of action would have to be taken, was marked by a singular event. I had crossed the valley early one afternoon with the idea of seeing Bernardo before collecting Chloë from the school bus. I can't remember why, because I had certainly put aside that time for writing, but no doubt I had some pressing neighbourly matters to discuss.

Cutting up from the valley, the path to Bernardo's winds through a wilderness of bushes, trees and cacti, enmeshed in climbers and creeping plants. There's a gravelly corner that squeezes between a steep cliff and a *chumbo*, or prickly pear; if you slip up here, you must make a split second decision on whether to roll down the cliff or fall into the *chumbo* and spend the next month extracting millions of microscopic barbs. This time I negotiated the corner without mishap, then panted up the last stretch to the road, where I found Bernardo gazing up into the branches of a tall fig tree that overhung the path.

He grinned ruefully at me and stroked the stubble of his upturned chin. I stopped beside him.

'*Hola Bernardo, que tal?*'

'Good morning, Cristóbal, it's okay, I don't complain. But I have a small problem here.'

'And what might that be?'

By way of an answer he indicated the crown of the fig tree. I looked up into the branches, shading my eyes from the sun with my hand. There was what appeared to be a small dog, high up in the tree. I looked quizzically at Bernardo.

'Yes,' he said. 'You see, it's der Moffli.'

'Yes, I can see it's the Moffli, but what on earth is it doing up in that tree?'

'He's dead,' said Bernardo with a certain solemnity.

'Ah,' I said, relieved to have found an explanation for the odd look of the dog, though this shed little light as to how it got up there. The Moffli was Bernardo's family pet, a little Pekinese dog, much beloved by the children. Initially there'd been two – called the Mofflis after a Dutch cartoon-strip – but the first had succumbed to some illness the year before, to the great distress of the children. And now it appeared that the other one had gone the same way.

'He died last night,' explained Bernardo. 'The last little Moffli. I didn't want the children to see him, so I decided to wait and throw him into the *barranco* while they were at school. Well, I swung him round and round, you know, like this' – he made a circular motion with his arm – 'and then I let him go... but I think I got the timing wrong.'

Bernardo looked away from the tree and turned towards me, and to our shame we both spluttered with laughter. Immediately Bernardo clamped a hand over his mouth and gestured me to hush. 'No, no – it's very sad,' he said, 'and a terrible problem. The tree is right over the path the children take from the school bus. Imagine how upsetting it would be if they looked up and saw the Moffli up there?'

As if on cue, Moffli lifted on a gentle zephyr and began to rock in his resting place. I could see now the gravity of it all.

'But how to get him down,' pondered Bernardo, 'before the children get home?'

'We could throw stones at him and see if we can knock him off,' I suggested.

Bernardo liked the idea, so we gathered a pile of rocks and set about hurling them at the unfortunate dog. Despite the odd lucky hit, gratifying in its way, the only effect was to push the Moffli even deeper into his cleft.

'No,' pronounced Bernardo at last. 'It's not working. We'll just have to think of something else.'

At that moment, the sound of an engine and a cloud of dust on the corner heralded the arrival of the school bus. I had a choice to make. I could run up to meet the children and improvise some distraction, or I could make myself scarce and loop down to meet Chloë at the bridge. I chose the latter.

Perhaps to atone for this outburst of un-neighbourly cowardice, I promised myself that I would write late into the night and continue working on the book all the way through the next day, an easy enough resolution to make while wandering back to the farm in the late afternoon. We had dinner and I retreated to the *cámara*. On the way I noticed the sheep had not yet returned to the farm: they were still out on the hillside behind the house. Night was falling and I began to worry about the risk of leaving them up there; there was a full moon and the creatures of the wild would be raving and seething with malevolence. The poor sheep, who seem more or less unaffected by the moon, wouldn't stand a chance. So I gathered a stick and Bumble and Big and stepped out up the hill.

The dogs raced happily into the scrub while I walked round the gentler gradients of the track, stopping every now and then to strain my ears into the silence, to try and catch the bongling of a bell. There was nothing and soon darkness fell. I trudged on up the rough track, my eyes adjusting to the faint light of the stars. Still not a sign nor sound of the sheep. Then the faint pallor that loomed over the high scarp to the east burst into the great glowing disc of the full moon, dazzling white against the blackness of the cliffs. The dogs hurtled to and fro, panting in the scrub, frightening partridges which rose hysterically into the air and clattered away down the hill. Bumble looked like a spectral dog, huge and white in the moonlight with her dark shadow moving beside her in the pale dust.

All of a sudden I heard a bell, distinct and near, no more than fifty metres off. I stood stock-still. Silence. The dogs came and stood beside me and together the three of us stood motionless, staring into the darkness. The bell was not repeated; the hill remained wreathed in silence.

We stood still, straining our ears for the slightest sound of the sheep. I breathed through my mouth – it makes less noise – and for a moment, instead of an enfeebled middle-aged European in glasses, I felt like a Masai warrior, lord of the hill before me and silent in the mountain night.

Soon, though, I grew tired of the warrior stance. There was the sound of dogs, barking in the distance, and I caught the wild cry of foxes way across the hill. I continued climbing, leaving the valley and heading for the pinewoods. This was bliss for the dogs, and I can think of few better ways to spend a moonlit night than wandering around in the mountains, but it was getting late, and I had already blown a night's work. Still, I could hardly sit and write while my sheep were being hunted around the mountainside by packs of lunatic wild dogs.

In spite of my misgivings, I finally had to admit that I was beaten. I had spent most of the night quartering the hill to no avail, and there was always the possibility – and it wouldn't be the first time – that the flock had cut round and taken another route back down to the stable.

The house was in darkness as I passed it. Ana had gone to bed. I continued down to the stable. There was absolute silence but as I bent down to peer through the window, this was broken by a shuffling and a bongle of a bell. There they were, the sods, safe in their beds. I remonstrated with them furiously, for wasting my night. 'Please, just don't do it again,' I pleaded. 'I'm trying to get something done which could be of some benefit to us all – new hayracks, a better class of grain, just think of it...' The sheep just looked at me, insolently chewing like yobboes in a yard.

The next day I slumped on my desk, exhausted from the night and a little demoralised. Perhaps I should forget this idea of becoming a writer. If the business of everyday living took up so much of my time – and that of course was a perennial problem of living in a remote *cortijo* – then how on earth would I find the extra time to do anything crea-tive? Soon the telephone would ring and it would be my friend and shearing partner José Guerrero, announcing the start of the shearing season: two months and more of solid grinding work that would leave me drained like a rusty bucket. It was as if a half-realised dream was already start-ing to vanish.

Then Ana came up with a solution. I should use the advance I'd been given to employ someone to help out on the farm. It was crazy to try and stretch myself, and wasn't that what an advance was for anyway, to buy me a little more time to write? It was a faultless idea that had only one fault. We didn't know anyone we could ask. Good farm labour is in short supply these days in the Alpujarras, and El Valero, being on the wrong side of the river, was not the most sought-after or social place to work.

'You should ask Manolo – he's a good worker,' said Domingo, whose advice I sought.

'Manolo del Molinillo, you mean?'

'Yes, there's nobody else as good, but you know that from when he helped clear out the *acequia* a couple of years ago with his father. And he's good with sheep, too.'

'I know Manolo well,' I said despondently, 'and I know what you're saying is true. But he's one person I can't employ...'

'Why not?'

'Well...' I began – I hadn't wanted to mention this – 'Manolo still hasn't paid me for that shearing I did for him last year.'

'I can't believe that of Manolo. There's not a drop of dishonesty in him...'

'That's what I used to think,' I said. 'Anyway, it's a bit difficult asking someone to work for you when they owe you money...'

'Not nearly as difficult as when you owe them money,' answered Domingo, before turning to go. He had some work he wanted to finish off in his studio.

MANOLO DEL MOLINILLO

PACO DE LA CHARCA – Paco of the marsh – lives between el Valero and Orgiva, in a *cortijo* which, as the name would suggest, is set in a marsh. He shares this unenviable terrain with three or four hundred sheep which root around eating a lot of water-mint and reeds and other bog-plants, as well as plenty of willow. I have shorn Paco's sheep for many years and have got to know him fairly well. He is not a true Alpujarreño, having moved here from Iznalloz, up in the hills to the north of Granada, but you'd not know it from his talk, which, when I'm around at least, seems to consist of fulminating against people from anywhere beyond the confines of Orgiva, and, in particular, foreigners.

'You come here and infest our land, murder our language! The Host! I can't understand a single word you say! You're good for nothing, apart from shearing sheep and you're not very good at that! Look at that sheep! What sort of shearing do you call that? I suppose you're going to charge me full rate for that one! You're thieves, all of you damn foreigners, robbing us poor natives blind.'

All this nonsense he delivers in a loud cracked rasping growl of a voice, that gets louder and more rasping as he warms to his theme, a cigarette clamped between the corner of his lips and eyes screwed into a shrewd stare. I used to think that he was serious, and the first time I sheared for him I was all for walking off the job. But Domingo, who was working alongside me, said Paco spoke to everyone like this, and it was meant to be good-humoured. And so it seems to be. I can now notice the signs of a smile playing around his eyes when he hurls the worst insults. Still, I appreciate he is an acquired taste.

Paco is only a couple of years older than me, but when I met him first, I had him down for at least sixty-five: the effect of the sun and the wind and the tobacco and the humours of the marsh and the relentless diet of pig-products – and a lot of shouting. A year ago, in fact, he suffered a mild heart attack that left him much weakened and even a little bit subdued.

Not long after this episode, I found him in the Bar Paraiso and he called me over in a voice that a normal person would use to hail a distant taxi but which was probably a decibel or two lower than his standard greeting.

'Cristóbal! Come over here and listen to my feeble whispering. I have a thing to tell you. I have sold my sheep.'

'What the hell are you going to do without your sheep, Paco? You'll go crazy.'

'I am worth nothing. I am no longer any good to anybody,' he continued, with a look of intent stoicism. 'And

I am going to devote myself more to the pleasures of the bottle. But listen – I've sold the sheep to Manolo.'

'You mean Manolo del Molinillo?'

'Yes – the same – the young one and that shit of a friend of his, Miguel. They have bought them off me for a very fair price and even now are out walking in the marsh with them. I want you to shear them.'

'Alright, I don't see why not. I know Manolo quite well. He's worked for me on occasions. He's a nice lad and good with the mules; but I can't really see him as a shepherd.'

'No, nor can I. And Miguel is too pig lazy. He won't be around to help him much. I predict a catastrophe. But they were the ones who wanted to buy them.'

Early one morning the next week I drove down the river-bed to La Charca and set up my gear in the pitiful shade of a half-dead olive tree in Paco's yard. Soon Manolo arrived, beaming with pride in his blue boilersuit at the head of his flock.

I got my head down and got stuck into the sheep, as Manolo caught them and plonked them effortlessly on the board beside me. Occasionally he would stop and look out for Miguel, who had promised to come and help him. Miguel, though, failed to show up and all day long Manolo made cheerful excuses.

It took two days of hard graft to get through the flock. At the end, as I packed up my machinery and stowed it in the car, Manolo confided: 'We haven't got the money on us at the moment, Cristóbal... can we pay next week?'

'Of course you can, Manolo,' I agreed. 'Don't you worry about a thing. Pay me whenever you can.'

In twelve years of shearing sheep in Spain I'd worked for some desperate characters, but I'd never had the least problem when it comes to payment, beyond a little creative counting. And I knew Manolo well. He was as straight as they come.

A month later I ran into Paco again. He was a lot better, and had dropped the whispering business. 'Hey, Cristóbal!' he began. 'Did you get the money for the sheep-shearing?'

'No, not yet, but it's only a couple of weeks...'

'They're not going to pay you anything!' Paco took to the role of shit-stirrer with relish.

'What do you mean?'

'Well, they made a cock-up of it all, just as I predicted, and now I've bought the sheep back off them. They're paying what debts they can – feed, grazing, labour and so on – but Manolo's been told not to pay the foreigner.'

This was something of a shock but I rallied as best I could. 'So, Paco,' I growled at him. 'If the sheep were yours before, and they're yours again now, and I've sheared them, then the one who owes me the money is you, because you're the one who will benefit from having them shorn, no?'

'Well,' smiled Paco, unfolding a grubby piece of paper from his pocket. 'Under other circumstances, maybe. But this piece of paper says that any debts incurred during the period of their ownership are their responsibility. So they're the ones who must pay you – and I can't see them doing it.'

Three hundred sheep, 150 pesetas a sheep – that was 45,000 pesetas – roughly two hundred pounds. It was money we could do with but, worse, there was the principle of the thing: it would be humiliating to be so deceived. So I rang Manolo up that evening, only to hear from his mother that he wasn't in; and it was the same the next night and the night after that. Soon I got fed up with ringing and hearing his mother's excuses, and fell into a sadness for my misjudgement.

A week or so after my chat with Domingo, Ana called me onto the terrace. She'd noticed a man on a horse threading his way up the riverbed towards our farm. We both squinted through the sunlight at the shape appearing and disappearing among the boulders. 'It's Manolo del Molinillo,' murmured Ana in surprise. Ana's sight is a lot keener than mine, but I could tell at once that she was right. Manolo is taller than most of the men around here and big-built, and he has such a relaxed and natural way on a horse that it's difficult to mistake him.

Sure enough, ten minutes later, Manolo was tethering his horse to a fencepost just below the house. I went down to meet him, adopting a cool, neutral expression which seemed all wrong for greeting a friendly type like Manolo.

He too seemed awkward and stared anxiously at the dust rather than greeting me with his usual open smile.

'Er... I've brought you something, Cristóbal.'

'Oh yes? What would that be?'

He handed me a great wad of notes. 'It's only half of the money I owe you and I'm sorry it's taken me so long, but times have been hard. We lost a pile of money on Paco's sheep, and I've had to work off the debt on my own. I've been working all the hours I can to get money to pay off our creditors, and it's been a lot of money. I'll bring you the other half just as soon as I can earn it, but there's not a lot of work at the moment.'

I was just ecstatic. I had known all along that there was no bad in Manolo and now the doubts were vanquished. I addressed him like a long-lost friend. 'Manolo, I knew you wouldn't let me down. Look, if you need more money you could always come and work for me... well, in fact, I could do with some help.'

Manolo was delighted with the offer, and over a beer or two we settled the deal. He also filled me in on the desperate weeks of shepherding, where he'd tried to keep the flock going on his own, only to discover that debts were closing in around him. He shuddered at the memory, then grinned even more broadly than before. He was going to settle in to regular work at El Valero while I, what was it I was going to do? Ah yes... I was going to sit up there in the *cámara* and write a book.

Manolo began work the day after our reconciliation, and we wandered down to the stable together to decide on the most urgent tasks. He stopped with a jolt, as he caught sight of our tractor. 'So, you've got a tractor,' he said, with barely-concealed excitement.

'Yup,' I said. 'A tractor.'

We were looking at a fifty-year-old Massey Ferguson 135, parked beneath an orange tree: a fine and serviceable machine it was, with little patches of bright red paint showing through the dust and rust. We'd bought it with some money left to us by Grum, as Ana's grandmother was known. The old girl was a hundred and four, and I think not entirely unhappy to slip off the mortal coil, though she might have preferred something daintier for us to remember her by.

For my part, I treated the tractor with a certain veneration, seeing in it a new agricultural beginning for El Valero. The only trouble was, I found it hard to pluck up the courage actually to drive the thing. Maybe it was the fact of being a father, or the extreme steepness of our farmland and all the tractor accidents that people so delighted in telling me about. Whatever, I felt very vulnerable indeed, a soft thing of flesh and brittle bone perched amid that exoskeleton of steel and awesome hydraulic power.

Manolo, by contrast, had no such reserve. Spellbound, he hopped onto the seat and impatiently began looking for the means to start it up.

'There's a black knob,' I explained. 'Push it in first and then turn the key.'

That was the first and last time I would have the ascendancy in tractor knowledge. From then on Manolo and the machine became as one. There was simply no tractor job that daunted him. The tractor had a front-end loader and with this Manolo set about transforming the landscape of our farm. He levelled the hideously rutted track that led to the house into a smooth and gently-contoured surface; he moved hitherto immovable rocks from where they had hindered cultivation; and with the cultivator, he tilled the earth on terraces so narrow that they hadn't been touched for years.

Through all this, Manolo worked with a pleasure that it did your heart good to see. Then one day the tractor decided to pack up in the middle of a field. Manolo was distraught.

We went to consult Domingo, who said it was the shear-bolt in the clutch housing. Manolo and I watched, hearts in mouths, as he skillfully replaced the broken bolt with a new one. 'You must be more gentle with it, Manolo,' he warned. 'If you don't take it a bit steadier, then a broken shear-bolt will be the least of your problems.'

We were both a bit worried by this and pressed Domingo for more advice. 'Less of the high-rev thumping and graunching,' he cautioned. 'You must treat her as if she were a woman.'

'Right. As if she were a woman,' mused Manolo with an uncertain smile.

It may have been a coincidence but from then on I began to notice Manolo paying small attentions to the tractor. The few parts that still had a chance of gleaming were rubbed with soft cloths and the engine was regularly nourished with oils. He bought for it a silver key-ring with a picture of San Isidro, the patron saint of farmers, and one morning arrived holding a colourful woollen cushion for the bucket-seat. Whenever he could, he would find some excuse to take the tractor home at night and cut a dash cruising up and down the Tíjolas strip.

For a time, I worried that the tractor had become an obsession, displacing Manolo's traditional skill as a mulet-eer. He has two mules as well as his beautiful young bay mare, and if anyone in the valley needs a heavy load hauled up to some impossible place, or a field ploughed on a near vertical hillside, it's Manolo they ask. With his *bestia* – the Spanish term for horses, mules and donkeys – he can perform delicate tasks beyond the capabilities of any farm machinery.

It would have been sad to see this skill lost. But we needn't have worried. Manolo had a special bond with his mules and he wasn't going to let them get out of condition. On summer evenings and at weekends, we would often pass him in the *vega*, working away with the *bestia*.

Meanwhile, I was attempting to carve out a new working life for myself. Towards the end of Manolo's first week on the farm, with Chloë despatched on the school bus, I headed up to the *cámara*, sat myself at the desk, opened my ruled exercise book and creased back the spine. The computer I'd just unpacked stood accusingly before me but I did my best to ignore it as I filled my pen. '*A la faena*,' I said to myself determinedly. 'On with the job...'

Within a few minutes, however, I found myself staring at the husking machine I'd moved into the corner of the room. I could imagine myself turning the big wooden handle until the great iron flywheel was humming round like a top, ready for some maize cobs to be slipped in. I could see the maize jiggling then hopping about a bit before suddenly disappearing among the gnashers inside the machine, sending a spray of yellow grain spattering from the nozzle into the basket. Surely there could be few better ways of spending an hour or two than sweating over the handle and watching the pool of grain grow in the bucket, while the heap of red-brown husks grew beside the machine, with the promise of a warm blaze on icy winter nights. The husks make wonderful firelighters.

I sighed, looked unenthusiastically at the cheap plastic computer, and then settled again to scribbling in my exercise book. A small wheel in the caverns of my brain creaked into action; I unscrewed my pen and wrote a short sentence.

Then I refilled the pen and listened to the sounds of the farm. I could make out Manolo chugging about on the tractor down by the eucalyptus tree, and reflected bitterly that chugging about the place on a tractor was where I wanted to be, rather than staring at a piece of paper, trying to earn money to pay Manolo to do it. Then the engine noise disappeared, and I could hear the cooing of the doves and the backdrop of a million cicadas.

The air inside the *cámara* became stifling as the midday sun toasted the thin concrete roof. Spreading my elbows wide on the desk, I laid my head on a cushioned bit of my upper arm and drifted away into a pleasant sleep. The next thing I knew, there was a whistling outside, and the door burst open with a resounding crash. Manolo stood there with a slightly bemused smile.

'*Tas escribiendo?* – you're writing?'

'Well, I'm trying to. What are you at down there?'

'I've ploughed the stable field and sown it with grass...'

'Have you harrowed it?'

'No, I'll bring the mules tomorrow for that. And I've watered the alfalfa – the pipes were blocked so I had to dismantle them all to get the muck out – clogged solid they were. It's that wind, it filled the *acequia* with sticks and leaves and oleander petals and they all got sucked into the pipe. When are you going to make that filter you keep talking about?'

'I'm sorry. I'll see if I can get round to it tomorrow...'

'*Bueno*. And I've rearranged the haystack and fixed the rams' water drinker and tied up the tomatoes...'

I looked at the piece of paper before me on the desk. Manolo was edging forward, trying to catch a glimpse of my morning's work. I covered it with my arm.

Manolo surveyed the room. 'Lots of books,' he observed.
'Yes, I suppose there are.'
'How's your book coming along, then?'
I looked down at my desk and thought of Manolo's awesome morning's achievements. On the piece of paper was written: *Chapter 1. Arrive at El Valero* – I took my pen and added a full stop. 'Not bad,' I lied. 'Not bad.'

At five or six o'clock, the heat begins to abate a little and the day's farmwork comes to an end. Manolo had come up to the house for a beer. We were sitting on the patio, Manolo surrounded by adoring dogs, patting them in turn with affectionate blows of the hand, me sipping mint tea beside him, discussing what we needed to do around the farm.

'You'll need to get some *abono artificial* to fertilise the alfalfa,' Manolo said.

'No, Manolo,' I replied. 'You know that we're registering as organic producers. So we can't use chemicals of any sort, nor *abono artificial*.'

'We'll put dung on, then...'

'Yes, dung and compost...'

'No *abono*, then? It does seem such a pity not to spread just a little bit of *abono*.'

'Look, Manolo. You know that people around here use far too many chemicals. It runs off into the river and poisons the fish. And the birds too. You remember what this place was like when you first used to come and clear the *acequia*. Romero had the place so soaked in poisonous chemicals that you never heard a bird sing – and now listen...'

We sat and listened. Mingling with the low roar of the river and the breeze in the eucalyptus were the songs of golden orioles, blackbirds, larks of one persuasion or another, and even a late nightingale.

'You don't hear birds singing in Tíjolas,' offered Manolo. 'And you're right, they get poisoned by the chemicals. Every day I find half a dozen dead birds.'

'Exactly – and it was just those birds that would have eaten the insects that destroy the crops. You need a balance between nature and agriculture, and once you start blasting the place with chemicals, you destroy that balance and the pests get out of control. And I think it's worth it to harvest just a little less of each crop simply for the pleasure of the birdsong.'

'It is. You're right... but it does seem a pity not to put just a little fertiliser on the alfalfa.'

We ordered a load of organic fertiliser to be shipped all the way from Barcelona, which mollified Manolo a bit. It was worm humus or some such thing – a sooty, powdery peat with apparently extraordinary powers of water retention, which is what you want here, because the water retention factor of our land is nil. A kilo of this stuff was supposed to retain ten litres of water.

I see my discussions with Manolo as a crusade for the planet. If we can convince him of the benefits of organic husbandry, then he will go down and preach to the village, and when Tíjolas falls, it won't be long afterwards that Tablones, Las Barreras, and even Orgiva may start to see things in a different light.

One day in June, it seemed as if the breakthrough had in fact come. Manolo thundered up the steps and burst through the fly- curtain. 'Look at this, will you?!' he gasped. He was cradling a huge and perfect melon. *'Vaya meloncillo!'* he enthused – what a lovely melonkin. 'And without a touch of *abono!'* he added, as if the whole thing had been his idea.

(Before I go further I ought to explain that one of the major idiosyncrasies of Spanish and particularly *Andaluz*, that variant of the language spoken in these parts, is the constant and excessive use of the diminutive, rendered by the suffixes *-ito* or *-illo*: a kind of equivalent to the English *-let* or *-kin* as in piglet or lambkin. But size isn't really the issue here, as it's more of an expression of enthusiasm for the object in question. Among country folk in particular this can get quite out of control. *Un vinillo*, a winelet, is not unreasonable as a snifter of wine, but *un vasito de agüilla*, a glasslet of waterkin? Needless to say, a whopping great melonkin barely counts as a contradiction in terms.)

That summer, as if to hammer home the organic message, we had our first bumper harvest of potatoes. All notion of other work had to be put aside, as we attempted to make the most of our vegetable bonanza. I found this a bit frustrating because I'd finally pulled my finger out and composed enough pages on the computer to send a disk to my publishing friends, and they were waiting for more. But the call of the potatoes was urgent, and each evening we devoted more and more time to bagging and washing the crop, hurling any blighted spuds into the *chumbo*. Ana and I worked together, with occasional help from Chloë, and as the evenings went by, stooped over piles of potatoes and bowls of vile water, we occasionally wondered if it was worth it. A potato sells for a peseta, or not much more, and we'd be lucky to bag a hundred potatoes an hour between us. It was, as you may imagine, dull and unrewarding labour, but that is what farming is all about. Potato after potato after potato, each washed in two changes of water and dried in the sun.

We stacked them in an outhouse, where it was dark and quite cool, and we set to making potato dishes to celebrate our home produce. Rosemary potatoes – blasted in the oven with oil, a whole bush of rosemary, garlic and olives; aligot – a light cloud of boiled spud puréed with cheese and cream and garlic and whipped until it has to be held down in the pan to stop it floating away; and we even tried a recipe for a pudding – essentially mashed potatoes with chocolate sauce – which was not a success.

And then the potatoes got blight. Pools of mephitic black muck appeared on the floor by the sacks, and when we tipped them out we recoiled in horror. A potato with the blight becomes an evil-smelling sludge. You poke a finger through the skin and it is like sewage. It makes you think of the misery of the Irish potato famine: the crowds of starving poor looking on in desperation as the clamps were opened, only to be met by a poisonous white ooze; and the thousands who lay dying green-mouthed from the grass they tried to eat while the fat ships sailed down the Liffey bursting with crates of food for export to the English. Market forces would save the day. A blighted potato puts me in mind of that...

Manolo, as if to compensate us for our misfortune with the potatoes, stepped up his gifts of food and fruit from his patch of land in Tíjolas. He would pick his way across the bridge laden with plastic bags of fresh goat's cheese, as well as tomatoes, onions, aubergines and the leathery local green peppers.

Manolo had become, if we stopped to think about it, a part of our family. As well as all his farmwork, he would also help with getting Chloë to and from school. I tended to do the morning run, and would occasionally combine it with a trip to the post office with the next instalment of the book, and Manolo would often meet the school bus at the end of the day. He used an old trail bike that a friend had left on the farm, and handled it like a horse, coaxing it skilfully around the boulders and dips in the river. My own technique was a bit reckless and had landed Chloë and me in the river on more than one occasion.

That summer Antonia had returned to Domingo's house from one of her short trips to Holland with an old family pet – an African Grey parrot called Yacko. Manolo was picking Chloë up on the motorbike when he heard about this newcomer and together they decided to go and pay it a visit.

The week before, Domingo had found on the road a spiky creature that he had never seen before. He had rolled it in a sack and taken it home. And then he had walked over to see if I had a clue as to what it might be. 'It's an *erizo*,' I said, rather pleased with myself for knowing the Spanish for a hedgehog, and I told him the usual stuff about feeding it on saucers of milk, and that it would be riddled with fleas. Domingo decided to adopt it.

When Chloë and Manolo got to Domingo's farmhouse, there was nobody about. They couldn't find the parrot but they did find the hedgehog. Like Domingo, Manolo had never seen a hedgehog before, and his notions about parrots were, understandably, sketchy. Together, he and Chloë stood peering at the creature, rolled as it was into a ball of prickles. 'Do you suppose,' asked Manolo quietly, 'that this is Domingo's parrot?'

Waiting For Juan

WANDERING UP TO THE HOUSE for a morning break, Manolo has a habit of whistling some utterly tuneless tune about three seconds before he bursts through the fly-curtain of our kitchen. The tune is a considerate warning but it is not quite enough to prevent me from being caught in the act – *in flagrante fregantis*, Ana calls it – or, up to the elbows in the washing-up. Manolo pauses, a blush of embarrassment spreading across his face as he gazes first at Ana reading a newspaper on the sofa and then at me soaked in suds at the sink.

'*Tas fregando..?*' he offers. 'You're washing up?'

'Yup,' I concur. '*Fregando...* washing up.'

He nods his head as if to register this anomaly.

Later at lunchtime, as often as not, Manolo will whistle again and arrive to find me standing at the stove.

'*Tas cocinando* – you're cooking?'

'Yup – *cocinando*,' I reply.

Now I love to cook. I consider it one of life's great pleasures, and one that can only be enhanced by constant practice, and I don't much mind washing a few plates and saucepans afterwards. Ana as it happens detests both jobs but has a peculiar tolerance towards tidying up, shopping and laundry, which I exploit to the full. And so we carve up the daily round in a reasonably equal manner.

This is not, however, the norm for Alpujarran men. When men work, they work like mules all day long, but when they finish that's it – they relax and have a drink and ease their aching limbs, while their wives, fresh from a round of chores, gardening and fieldwork, wait on them. Of course there are some men who might help out in the garden, do their bit with the childcare, or even try a few culinary ideas – witness Domingo's jam making. But this is fairly unusual stuff. It would take a brave man to interrupt talk of hunting or water rights in a village bar with a new recipe for chestnut soufflé.

To be honest, a part of me withers whenever Manolo catches me in the kitchen. There's a certain tone to his '*tas fregando* that makes me question myself, wonder if all is as it should be in the masculinity stakes. Not that Manolo says anything specific, mind you, but his tone and slightly shamed look has a peculiarly crumpling effect. He reminds me, I fear, of my own reactions to Eduardo, a fundamentalist fruitarian who squats in a half-built house in the *vega* of Tíjolas. Eduardo is a fundamentalist in that he not only survives exclusively on fruit, but only eats windfalls; 'the tree must give its fruit without the duress of plucking,' as he puts it. As you might imagine, this is hardly a strengthening diet, and if the trees are unusually generous then he has to ferry his trawl home in small sacks like an ant carrying scraps from a leaf.

None of this should matter, except there are odd moments in life when a macho reputation does have some use. For instance, on the summer after my return from Sweden, when word got round that Juan Gallego, a local shepherd, had got it into his head to murder first his ex-lover and then me.

This episode began one July evening on the road outside Orgiva. I was standing by the car, talking to a cousin of Manolo's, when suddenly there was a yelling and shouting and a woman came stumbling round the corner in a state of hysteria.

'Please help,' she babbled in Spanish. 'He's going to kill her – he's gone really crazy – go now, please..!'

'Wait,' I said. 'Tell me what you want me to do and where and what's happening...'

'Just go, now, please, over there!' she implored.

So I got in the car and headed off in the direction the woman had indicated, wondering what on earth I was letting myself in for, but knowing I had to go anyway. After about a kilometre I came across two people standing by the side of the road. One was Petra, a slight Danish woman with long, light brown hair, which she had swept in front of her face in a vain attempt to hide behind it. The other was her lover Juan, a man I knew a little as a result of having sheared his sheep a few times. Though barely taller than Petra, Juan seemed somehow to be towering over her with a look of clenched menace.

Petra acknowledged my arrival with a terrified glance. 'Please don't leave me alone with him, Chris, he's going to kill me.'

'Cristóbal, what are you doing here?' demanded Juan with a look of fury.

I got out of the car and Petra explained as well as she could what was going on. 'I'm leaving him, Chris. I can't stand his moods and his wildness any more. And he can't accept that I'm leaving like this so he keeps grabbing me and shaking me and trying to make me say I'll stay. And now he says he's going to kill me – we've called the police but just please don't leave me alone with him. Stay till the police get here.'

Petra was crying now and rubbing her bruised arms. 'Okay,' I said. 'I'll stay until you tell me I can go.'

All this we said in English. It didn't seem necessary somehow to translate it for the benefit of Juan.

'What are you saying? Speak Spanish,' he shouted.

'Petra is telling me what's going on and I'm staying here until she says I can go,' I said to Juan.

'You can go now. I don't want you here.'

'No. Here I stay till Petra says I can go,' I repeated.

Juan bristled – a stocky man, with teeth mostly knocked out, nose well broken and a stubbly moustache. He muscled up to me. I held my ground.

'Cristóbal, a man does not get in the way of another man and his woman,' he snarled.

'He does, Juan, when there is violence, so here I stay.'

Little by little, as our group moved back and forth between the house, from which Petra was getting her belongings, and the van where she was stowing them, Juan began to get aggressive with me. He didn't hit me, but there was a lot of the pushing and shoving with chest puffed out that men do as a prelude to slamming their fists into each others' faces. 'We used to be friends, Cristóbal,' Juan growled. 'But now you have a serious enemy.'

Anyway, I did my stuff and stuck to Petra like glue, and after about half an hour a Guardia Civil patrol car appeared and two policemen got out. One was a pleasant-faced young man who was obviously a trainee, the other a little runt of a man with a thick grey moustache and a strut like a bantam-cock.

'Show me your papers, passport...' he snapped at Petra. 'And you,' he turned to me. 'What are you doing here?'

'I'm staying to make sure that my friend doesn't get hurt.'

'Well, you can clear off now,' he said, with a look of distaste.

'I'm staying until this woman says I can go,' I told him with what I hoped was an answering sneer. It was immediately obvious that this noble little custodian of the law thought that if Juan wanted to beat up his girlfriend then that was his own affair and none of us should be interfering.

The bantam disappeared into the house with Petra to check her papers, and Juan and I were left outside in the dark with the young apprentice. Juan was still being aggressive towards me. 'You're not going to arrive home alive tonight, Cristóbal,' he said. 'Juan,' I warned him. 'It's all very well to threaten a man, but to do it in front of the Señor Guardia here is surely foolishness, no?' I was a little emboldened by the young policeman's cosh and his gun and his silly green hat.

In the end the Guardia escorted Petra to the police station, and as she left she assured me that she had friends who would collect her and that she would be alright.'Thanks, Chris,' she said. 'I'll be fine now.'

I drove home. Ana and I sat outside eating a late supper, as you do on hot summer nights, while Chloë dozed on the sofa. Halfway through the meal, the phone rang. Ana answered it. 'I want to speak to Cristóbal' said an angry voice. Ana passed me the telephone. '*Diga* – speak,' I said, only to hear the phone slammed down. 'That'll be Juan,' I confided. 'Checking to see if I'm at home so he can come round and kill me.'

The call somehow put a damper on the rest of the meal. We lapsed into silence and you could hear the clinking of the cutlery and the burbling of wine being poured into glasses. At midnight, Ana rose from the table. 'I'm sure it'll be alright, Chris, but give me a shout if you hear anything worrying,' she said, as lightly as she could manage, then gave me a surprisingly tender goodnight kiss and took herself and Chloë off to bed. I repaired to the roof, where I often slept on hot summer nights, and placed a mattock beneath my bed.

Now, a mattock is a pretty uncompromising tool. A good blow to the head would be likely to end in serious injury or death. Still, I reckoned if Juan were going to make the effort to come all the way out here in the middle of the night, he was not just coming to bring me a bunch of flowers. He was going to fix me good. He had seemed just as much riled by my role in the evening's episode as over the loss of Petra. Pride was at stake.

One of the odd things about this event was that I felt a kind of guilt, as if I had offended some base animal instinct and that Juan was right to seek to duff me up or worse. I wondered how I would have felt had the situation been reversed. Surely I would have been glad to have someone there stopping me throwing punches – I mean, once I'd calmed down? Wouldn't I? I'd have given a lot to know at that moment whether Juan was of the same mind.

The roof I had chosen as summer bedroom has a sweeping view of all sides and is set a little higher than the rest of the house. Juan would not be able to see me in my bed unless he had decided to creep up from behind, but that would mean a very long, very deliberate tramp over the mountains. The moon was not far off the full so I would see my enemy long before he saw me – assuming, that is, that I didn't fall asleep.

What should you wear in bed when you're waiting for someone to come and kill you? It was a hot night and what I usually wear on a hot night is nothing. But it wouldn't do to have to pull on clothes as a prelude to defending myself, while a naked man wielding a mattock is a far from formidable looking opponent. I decided on a tee-shirt and underpants as my battle costume, with a pair of sandals ready to slip on, under the bed by my weapon.

I lay down on my back and looked up at the bright sky. It was too light to sleep like that, so I rolled over and peered over the pillow at the moonlit rivers and valleys. I tried to breathe quietly so I could hear any furtive footfalls above the quiet swish of the river. Then I got fed up lying that way and rolled over again giving the mattock a quick fingering just to make sure.

It was a bad business, this. It seemed such unwarranted bad luck to find myself preparing to fight for my life in my underpants with a mattock on a rooftop in the moonlight.

Life, which had hitherto seemed pretty good, suddenly seemed even sweeter. I fingered my mattock again and rolled over. There was a car creeping into the valley. I could see the lights in the dark rocks above La Herradura. This was it. It was late; who else would be coming in at this time of night? I had a good fifteen minutes till he got here, assuming that he left his car on the other side of the river – and he would do that because he would hardly drive all the way up to the farm and thus lose what he believed was the advantage of surprise.

I slipped into my trousers, buckled my sandals and grabbed the mattock, then I sat on the bed for a bit. All was silence now; the car had disappeared into the valley. I weighed up the mattock. Now, how do you hit a man with a mattock? Do you crack him over the head with the back of it? Or do you go for no holds barred, finish him off in one, cleave the bastard down through the middle with the blade?

I wasn't sure, but probably the technique would become clear as the combat heated up. I crept up the hill to look over to the river bridge. I just caught the lights heading off up the track to Carrasco. Not Juan at all, some midnight visitor for our neighbours across the river.

Back to bed. I thought about Petra and Juan. I had thought their affair was romantic – but maybe not. Petra was a generous soul, sexy and optimistic and always game for something interesting. She had come out to Orgiva after growing tired of an office job in Copenhagen, and fallen in with a Spanish-Moroccan bloke from Ceuta. Together they travelled back and forth to Morocco, trawling for artefacts which they would sell at a stall in the market. Then Paco, the partner, decided he was going to India to do some work on his karma, while Petra took up with an installation artist and part-time welder, whom she had met in Alicante. All seemed to go well for a while and she would return in high spirits with her new lover to stay with friends in the mountain villages. And then one day, I was out wandering in the hills of the Contraviesa when I found myself in the middle of a big flock of sheep. Standing at the back, tending them with a stick and a couple of scruffy-looking dogs, was Petra – the very same Petra who had once worked as a stationery buyer for a mobile phone company.

The sheep, she said, belonged to Juan. I knew Juan a little and had found him a quiet, reserved sort of a man. I liked him. Petra went on to tell me how she had cast her lot with him and moved into his ramshackle *cortijo* to share the shepherd's life. Sometimes I would come across her in town in her van, loading up with sacks of feed and shepherd's necessities. And then she told me how the two of them had left the flock in the charge of a cousin or two, and headed off round Spain in the van for a holiday – a thing Juan never would have dreamed of doing before.

So, all in all, it seemed that Petra enriched Juan's life, and Juan and his pastoral existence was really something of a revelation to Petra. 'Oh, it's wonderful, Chris,' she would tell me eagerly. 'It's opened out a whole new world for me. I can't tell you the pleasure I get from living up on the mountain with the sheep, getting to know this new way of life.' Her eyes would glisten with excitement as she said this, so I knew it was so.

And now here I was, alone in the moonlight with my mattock, waiting for Juan, who was on his way to kill me. I couldn't help but feel disillusioned about it all. I rolled over and listened to the sounds of the night. An insect hummed, another whined and stopped near my ear. A scops owl started its monotonous booping from the river – boop... boop...boop – a noise to drive you to distraction. Ana's Aunt Ruth from Brighton came to stay with us one weekend. 'Are you sure there's not a factory of some sort around here?' she had asked, peering fearfully into the unrelieved blackness of the mountain night. 'Not as far as we know,' said Ana acidly. 'But that noise,' said Ruth, 'it sounds so like people clocking off.'

I listened to the scops owl and thought a bit about Aunt Ruth's visit. She had enthused about the farm: 'How wonderful to live so wild and free in the mountains, drinking water from the spring, so far from the hurly-burly, the hustle and bustle, well out of the rat-race, and not stuck in the concrete jungle in an endless traffic jam.' She hooked one cliché after another. Later we discovered she had so feared the water from the spring that she had cleaned her teeth in lemonade.

I fell asleep for a while, but all of a sudden I was aware of the dogs barking furiously – the intruder-bark. Back into the trousers, grab the mattock, feel around for my glasses by the bed-leg. The dogs were going crazy; somebody was lurking around the house. This was it. 'Right, you bastard! Come and get it!' I said out loud to myself, taking courage from the ring of these words and their sense of impending violence. I peered down from the roof. Nothing, not a sound. Still the dogs were at it, infuriated by some presence.

And then I heard it. It was the call of a fox in the valley, that little howl of feral yearning, the distillation of all the wildness, savagery and horror of the night, a call that thrills your very blood – and drives the dogs bonkers. It's the call of the wild and it makes the dogs feel guilty of a moral dereliction as they slumber on the rug by the fire. It reminds them of the way they should be – not consorting with cats, slurping dog-food and biscuits for breakfast, and walking to heel on the end of a lead. 'Come to me,' the fox calls, 'this is how life should be lived, racing through the woods on starlit nights, massacring runs of obese hens, delighting in their cries of terror. Come on, you unfit, molly-coddled slobs, come and get it.' Of course it drives the dogs to distraction.

I returned to my bed, almost regretful at the lack of action. And sleep did not come easily. The night was just too exciting and, besides, if Juan did succeed in sticking me with his knife, then this might be the last night I would ever see. It seemed a pity to waste it in sleep.

The moon moved on down and slipped behind Cerro Negro, 'Black Hill', and the sky filled with stars. I gazed up at the Milky Way, and remembered when I was a child lying awake and listening to the terrors of night, the shifts and cracks made by my parents' old house, or more probably by fearful fiends and things too horrible to name who were inching their way out from under the bed. I was always a little surprised to see the sun shining through the curtains in the morning, and to know I had made it through yet another night. But over the years I became accustomed to surviving, and this was the first night for a long time that I had been unsure of.

As I considered the stars in those dark hours that come before dawn, I began to feel a little more confident of making it through to morning. And then I heard him – of course, he would choose the darkest hour. He was creeping through the bushes on the hill above me. He could see me from there before I saw him. I froze with fear, fished again for my glasses and waited shivering by the bed, hefting the mattock. I could hear his breath, he was that close. Then a careful footfall and the breaking of a bush. I gripped the mattock hard. I heard him cough – and then an enormous fart. No man could fart that loud, not even the formidable Juan. It was Lola, the horse, and now I could hear her munching happily amongst the rosemary.

A distant cock crowed and then another, and the scops owl stopped booping. The sunlight filtered through, a fly settled on my nose, and I knew it was morning. Juan wouldn't come now. He didn't come the next night either.

I told Manolo about the business and he looked earnestly at me. 'Juan?' he said. 'Juan! You don't want to mess with Juan – he's a maniac. He kills people for fun! You know he killed old Pepe Díaz, don't you? He's known for fighting – even the Guardia Civil are frightened of him – well, they're frightened of everybody but they're particularly frightened of Juan. He carries a *navajón* – a ten-inch knife – in his boot. He's bad news. Cristóbal, you're in real trouble now.'

'Thanks,' I replied. 'That's very reassuring. How do you know all this, anyway?'

Manolo rolled his eyes. 'I worked for Juan last year, mucking the dung out of his sheep-stables. He's a strong bastard. He could lift a mule up with one hand. And he has a terrible temper – I'd sooner mess with a wild boar than with that Juan.'

'Still,' I replied, keeping a front of optimism. 'He didn't come and get me last night, nor the night before. I don't think he'll bother to come and kill me now. I may have got away with it...'

'Oh, I wouldn't count on that. He'll probably get you at the Feria – the summer fair. That's when these things are done here. He'll be drunk and spoiling for a fight and he'll be furious about losing his blonde. Yes, Feria's when he'll get you.' Manolo smiled happily at me.

Orgiva Feria – the town's big festival – was the following week. The business with Juan might make it a little more interesting than usual. Feria is a time of unbelievable cacophony, when the townsfolk go overboard indulging their passion for noise. There's a fairground where each and every ride has its own sound system, each more ear-splitting than the last. The streets are lined with brightly-lit sweet stalls and lottery stalls where you can win polyester day-glo cuddly toys, and these too have their own music, pumped out at about ten times the decibel level that strikes you stone deaf. The bars in the plaza, meanwhile, have sound systems the size of small houses, which thunder and rattle day and night, making it impossible to hold the faintest trace of conversation. Yet the locals just sit there chatting away as though nothing were happening. It's my belief that the Spanish have better evolved ears than the rest of us.

As if the noise isn't enough, Feria is also the time of year when the wind gets up. It comes trickling over the top of the Contraviesa, building up speed as it races through the gullies and canyons, then roars uphill from the Seven-Eye Bridge and howls into town, carrying plastic bags and beercans before it. It moans and wails round every corner, thick with grit and gravel which stings your eyes and gets in your nose and sets your teeth on edge as you eat the public paella in the plaza.

The only saving grace of the Orgiva Feria is the *pinchito* stall, where you can lean against the tin bar hour after hour, munching your way through spicy skewers of pork and drinking warm dry sherry from a paper cup. It's the thought of this – and the fact that Chloë enjoys hanging out at the fair with her schoolfriends – that keeps me going back each year. And besides, this Feria I had to show my face. I wasn't going to let myself be bullied into missing the festive delights by some homicidal shepherd... even if he could lift a mule with one hand, and even if he did carry a ten-inch *navajón*.

Almost as soon as Ana, Chloë and I arrived in town, I spotted Juan chatting with a couple of friends in the street. I was all for stepping over to him straight away and giving my masculinity an airing, but Ana made this impossible by walking off and leaving me with Chloë. A smart move. She knew I wouldn't consider a brawl the most edifying spectacle for my six-year-old daughter.

After Chloë had gone off with her friends, I settled down for a stint at the *pinchito* stall, and waited to run into Juan. Manolo and Domingo were both at the bar, and Domingo comfortingly assured me that Juan reckoned I had been Petra's lover – why else would I interfere? – and that his anger was still festering.

Juan, however, didn't show up again.

In the town a few weeks after Feria I ran into Petra for the first time since the night of violence. She embraced me warmly.

'For Chrissake lay off, Petra!' I said, backing off. 'You want to try and get me killed again?'

'No, don't worry about it, Chris. I just wanted to thank you for being so wonderful that night.'

'It's all very well to say "Don't worry", but there's a dangerous maniac out there with a big knife and if he sees his blonde all over me in the high street then I'm meat.'

'Oh, Juan is alright. He's not a dangerous maniac at all. In fact I must rush because I'm just going to pick him up and take him to hospital...'

'You what?!'

'He's got kidney stones and the pain makes him crazy. That was partly what made him so aggressive that night; he was crazy with pain and I had refused to take him to hospital.'

'Petra, why on earth didn't you say any of this then?' I asked, appalled.

'Perhaps I was wrong that night. Juan is usually as gentle as a lamb. Anyway I must fly. Bye!'

I told Manolo what Petra had said. 'Oh – Juan is alright,' he said. 'He wouldn't hurt a fly. He didn't actually kill Pepe Díaz either, it was a heart attack. No, there's no doubt about it, Juan wouldn't have harmed you.'

I looked at him sideways.

'And what about the *navajón* he keeps in his boots?' I asked.

'I wouldn't know about that,' he answered with a smile. 'I've never had any cause to look inside them.'

TELEPHONY

S O FAR AT EL VALERO we have resisted the call of the
mobile phone. Its appeal is admittedly limited,
since a mobile wouldn't work where we live,
surrounded as we are by a ring of mountains. But
I'm a little uneasy in any case with telephone technology;
I once wasted a morning trying to make a phone call from
a friend's house using the TV remote control. Ana, too,
is something of a Luddite. She won't have anything to do
with computers, for example. Not long ago, someone gave
her an old IBM golf-ball typewriter which is as big and
heavy as a small traction engine. She was delighted with
it even though it spatters any paper that passes through
it with gobbets of light engine oil. 'This is the future,' she
announced as she heaved the thing through the doorway.

For many years we had no phone at all at El Valero. We
wrote letters to our friends and received letters in return,

and on the odd occasion when there was something pressing, we would go to the telephone-house in Tíjolas. An
enterprising family in the village had invested in a telephone
meter. This enabled them to provide a public service and,
with an astronomical multiplication of the already ruinous
Telefónica rate, to turn a nice profit. However much they
charged, though, the telephone-house was not a place for
a relaxed call. The phone and its meter were mounted on
the wall of the family sitting room, between a picture of the
Bleeding Heart and a bunch of faded plastic flowers. Callers
were clearly intruders on family life.

The quickest way to get to the telephone-house in those
days was to trek down the river, the road being particularly
bad. So a telephone call became quite a performance. First
there was the bracing hour-long walk, crashing through the
cane brakes and sloshing thigh-deep in fast-flowing water.
Then there was the problem of insinuating yourself into a
stranger's home and trying not to drip river water onto the
scrubbed floor.

The usual routine was to announce your arrival with
a shout – or, at least that's what the locals would do. I
tended to be a bit hesitant, asking in excessively formal
language 'if perhaps I might make use, for a short time,
of the telephone.' The telephone-woman would then
look me up and down disapprovingly, lingering with
particular distaste on my sodden shoes, before gestur-
ing with an imperious motion that I was to follow her
through the fly-curtain. Once inside the gloomy sitting
room, she would click the meter back to nought and then
stand beside it, arms folded, glaring at me. On a really
bad day, other members of the family would gather and
glare, too.

As I dialled the exotic foreign number, I would stand tight to the wall and grin vacuously at the watchers as the phone rang away at the other end of the line. It would ring and ring – Telefónica gives you a minute – then stop. For the full minute everybody would stare at me.

'No reply,' I'd say to the telephone-woman.

'He didn't get a reply,' she'd translate for the benefit of the others. They'd grunt at the news and shuffle out.

And then I would head back up the river, jogging and leaping rocks to try and get back before nightfall.

Ana and I made do with letters and the Tíjolas telephone-house for our first six years in Spain – including the time of Chloë's birth, which in retrospect may have been a bit rash. But we were happy enough with the arrangement and agreed that life was probably better without a phone – even if we could have had one, which we couldn't. For Telefónica, a corporation with little zest for philanthropy, was not going to run a land line all the way out to the valley and across the river just for us.

Then one early summer's day in Granada we passed a shop promoting a new type of radio telephone. We went in to take a look and, like a couple of country bumpkins, were signing up before we knew it. It seemed almost too good to be true. We could purchase a brand new radio handset and base at a special price, grant-aided for outlying rural properties, and within a week an engineer would come to see about installing it.

And so he did, arriving hot and flustered after the walk from the bridge and complaining that the battery on his receiving apparatus was flat. He grumbled around the place for a further half hour, doing all that he could to make us feel guilty for the inconvenience we were causing him by our decision to install a telephone in a remote *cortijo*. He seemed to grow crosser by the minute until, finally, he pronounced, like some terrible indictment: 'No, it won't work. There's no signal anywhere in the house. You're just too far from everywhere.'

'But you just said your battery was flat,' I pointed out.

'*Claro* – but that has nothing at all to do with it', he growled. 'Wait, there is just a faint signal right over there – it's almost too feeble to hear but it's the best you're going to get out in this godforsaken place. This spot right here is where you must have your telephone.' He looked at us with a sort of triumph.

'We can't put a telephone there,' we gasped. 'That's right in the middle of the *chumbo*.'

Now, the *chumbo* (or more properly *chumbera*) is a prickly pear, a plant that adorns almost every *cortijo* in the peninsula. In the sixteenth century, when it was brought back along with agaves and gold and silver from the Americas, it was discovered not only to have tasty fruit but to have the extraordinary property of absorbing shit. The *chumbo* became an essential component of every country property, and it is a convenience rural folk find hard to give up. Last year a shepherd in Torvizcón, up the Cádiar river, showed me around his newly-modernised *cortijo*. Proudly he opened every door and displayed all the innovations: the TV, the chandelier, the fitted kitchen, until with a flourish he opened wide the door to the lavatory: 'And here,' he said, 'is the toilet, with running water and everything. We fitted it last year' – he looked at me to check that I was paying attention – 'but thanks be to God, we have not yet had to make use of it!'

So, although there's much to be said in favour of the *chumbo*, it's not an obvious place for a telephone. I had imagined, perhaps foolishly, that we might be able to have the telephone in the house, but it was clearly not to be. 'What you must do,' said the engineer, 'is build a construction – a sort of box – which can house the receiving apparatus.'

A telephone-box in the garden. Well, that did have a certain appeal and we set to discussing its construction the moment the engineer went off on his way. Ana was particularly keen. 'If you are going to build a telephone receiving box out in the *chumbo*,' she suggested, 'then why not combine it with something more useful – like, say, a dog kennel?'

'Why not indeed? Could it be a domed dog kennel do you think?' I had always wanted to build a dome.

'Whatever shape you like,' said Ana who was pleased to have a dog kennel of any stamp – with flying buttresses, if necessary.

So I started on the domed dog kennel. But of course after a certain height the bricks started to fall inwards, and – despite looking for inspiration in a book on Istanbul, with pictures of the great mosque of Aghia Sophia – I grew disheartened, and flattened it off. The final result looked rather like a fairy mushroom, or the bottom floor of a truncated pagoda.

Two weeks later a new Telefónica engineer turned up. He was an altogether different man, a keen pigeon fancier, and with a full battery on his tester, which endeared him to me right away.

'What on earth is that?' he asked as he arrived, looking at the dog-kennel thing.

'That's the construction for housing the telephone receiving apparatus,' I said proudly.

'Good God, man, you can't have a telephone there!' He looked at me in astonishment. 'It's right in the middle of the *chumbo!*'

I told him about his predecessor with the flat battery.

'Well, according to my meter, you can put the thing right here where we're talking, slap bang in your kitchen... yes, that's as good a signal as you'll need.' And he pointed to the wooden beam above the window, the ideal place for a phone. He wandered around the place a bit more for good measure, in case he could find a better signal anywhere else. Luckily he couldn't.

'Those are beautiful *palomas* you've got up there,' he said, looking at the pigeons on our roof.

'They're lovely, aren't they?' I boasted. 'They're fan-tails.' And as if on cue they began flopping about on the roof.

'I can see that,' he said. 'I like fan-tails, but they're hopeless fliers, you know. I keep pigeons at home and I've got some wonderful fliers. I'll bring you a few, if you like. Your telephone will start playing up in a week or so. I'll bring the pigeons when I come and fix it.'

That night we celebrated the arrival of the new telephone by phoning my mother in England. Now, I've phoned my mother on countless occasions but rarely had I been so struck by the phenomenon of her voice appearing in my ear in another part of the world. It seemed incredible that I could chat to her while peering out of the doorway at our very own mountains and rivers. I could tell that she was similarly moved by the occasion. 'Is that Chloë in the background? Good heavens, there's Bonka!' she exclaimed excitedly.

Next we rang Bernardo over on the other side of the valley. He had just installed one of these new contraptions too, so we rang to compare notes and offer mutual congratulations on our giant step into the future. La Cenicera, Bernardo and Isabel's *cortijo*, is barely a kilometre away as the crow flies, and with the wind in the right direction you can shout across. Yet that night he might as well have been a mile underwater. We did our best for five minutes then plonked down the receiver, without having managed to glean even one word of Bernardo's side of the conversation – if indeed it was Bernardo on the phone.

When Enrique the engineer turned up the following week to fix the phone, which had surpassed his prediction by packing up altogether, he came with a large cardboard box tucked under his arm. Inside were a couple of exquisite, white straight-tailed pigeons. We shut them in with our fan-tails for a week so they could get used to their new home, and then let them out. This was a revelation, for these *palomas* really knew how to fly. They launched together off the roof and soared out into the plains of shimmering air above the valley, far out over the river towards the hills beyond. Then, shining white against the deep blue sky and dark mountains, they raced each other back, winged up over the acacia and settled on the roof. Then off they set to do the whole thing again. It was exhilarating to watch them.

'Our fan-tails don't fly at all,' said Ana. 'They're avian slobs. To think we might never have known what proper pigeon flight is!'

The Telefónica pigeons were inseparable and flew together farther and farther away, while the fan-tails ignored them completely, keeping up their cooing and flopping routine. After a time, though, it seemed the fliers were trying to encourage the slobs. The fan-tails would spend all day lined up on the edge of the roof in a long line – all of them who were not busy sitting on eggs in the coop below – and the flyers wandered calmly up and down behind them, pushing them off the roof and blocking them from landing again. A few of them did try some slightly more daring flights, even venturing over to the eucalyptus. As it happened, however, caution would have been a better option. The high-profile flights of the new pigeons attracted the attention of eagles, and one by one we started to lose the fan-tails. The Telefónica pigeons were too fast for the eagles, and too quick on the turn – but the poor fan-tails were easy prey.

One day, though, there was only one Telefónica pigeon; the eagles had finally managed to get his friend. The survivor was desolate, and pined for days, sitting miserably by himself and occasionally going for short, lonely flights, but with little spirit left. We didn't mind losing the odd fan-tail; it kept the population under control, and I have to admit that it was pretty exciting to see the Bonelli's eagles so close to the house. However, we were deeply saddened by the loss of the Telefónica pigeon. We felt we had lost something of beauty from our lives.

And then one morning I was out early, rowing up the oats and vetches in the river fields, when suddenly a whoosh of wings in the sky made me look up. There was a great gang of fan-tails with the Telefónica pigeon at their head, setting out on a long flight to the far end of the valley.

At long last he had managed to persuade them, and now he had company to fly with.

Our visits from Enrique the engineer continued, but sadly he never managed to recreate with his tweaking of our phone system anything like the easy reach across the valley that the *palomas* had achieved. Bernardo still sounded as if he was talking from a deep sea trench.

One day, Bernardo and I were discussing this singular phenomenon, sitting on the stump of a fig tree by the spring, when Domingo chanced by on Bottom, his donkey.

'You ought to get one of these wireless phones like we've got,' said Bernardo, a little surprisingly.

'Yes, you really should,' I agreed, falling into line.

'What use have I for such a thing?' said Domingo, lurching to a stop. 'I don't know anyone to telephone, and even if I did, what would I say to them?'

We all considered this for a moment before Domingo added: 'Anyway, I'm more interested in those new things, you know those things that go inside the computer...' Bernardo and I stared back at him blankly.

'Disks?' I volunteered.

'No – modems,' he replied. I hadn't, at that time, the first idea what a modem was, and judging from Bernardo's fixed smile neither had he. Without realising he was out on a limb here, Domingo treated us to a resumé of the joys of surfing the Internet, and the difficulty we were going to have getting wired in the Alpujarras. Antonia was keen, apparently, to exhibit some of their sculptures online, but it would take a new generation of mobile phones and a laptop to stand a chance of getting it working. Bernardo seemed to be agreeing, though his broad smile still wasn't giving anything away.

'With new technology it pays to wait,' Domingo continued.'The quality and price always improve. Buy the first lot that come on the market and you'll find it's almost always crap.'

'*Es verdad* – that's true,' we both mumbled.

Bottom twitched her ear to remove a fly, and looked at us thoughtfully, then, following an imperceptible command from Domingo, moved off at a trot. Bernardo and I stayed on the fig-stump for a bit in silence, and watched our neighbour disappearing down the road. We were neither of us in a hurry to resume the discussion about modems. I tried another tack.

'Sometimes it's better than others,' I offered.

'What is?' asked Bernardo.

'The telephone – sometimes it's bad, sometimes it's very bad.'

'And sometimes it doesn't work at all,' he concluded.

'Yup, that's right.'

'Somebody once told me why that is,' said Bernardo. 'Apparently the satellite has got a broken wing and now has to limp around in the sky like a three-legged dog.'

We sat a little bit longer, absorbing the full impact of this information until Bernardo noticed that the goats were getting dangerously close to his vegetables, and we brought our technological deliberations to a close.

In those first heady days our heads hummed with telephony and we were open to almost any idea of signals zinging their way across the stratosphere. It's the only way that I can begin to explain why a secular-minded citizen, in sound mind and not under the influence of any drug, should wake up one morning convinced that he was hearing celestial music.

It happened within just a few weeks of installing the phone. On a morning almost indistinguishable from any other that dry, hot, cloudless summer, I woke to find the valley faintly ringing with a curious droning and humming sound. It certainly seemed unearthly, and had an awesome quality, as if the sound were emanating from the very rocks and hills. I woke Ana and asked if she thought it might be the Final Trumpet. I could tell she was unnerved by the way she listened intently for a while and then answered my question. Normally her first words are about tea.

'Well, it doesn't sound much like a trumpet to me. It's more of a low drone,' she concluded. I tried to argue that a celestial trumpet was hardly going to sound like the wind section of some seaside brass band but she seemed to have lost interest. Then the phone rang, unusually for such an early hour. It was someone blowing bubbles through a snorkel. We took it to be Bernardo ringing to see if we'd heard the noise too and if we knew anything about it. The whole valley it seemed was full of this sound, and as far as I knew, it was filling the whole world.

'I think one of us ought to investigate,' I said decisively, and pausing only to make myself decent (though in the circumstances nakedness might have been appropriate) I set out in search of the source of this phenomenon. First I walked down the track to the river and scoured the terraces and fields, then I crept down towards the riverbed and out through the tamarisk wood. Everywhere the sound was the same, neither louder nor softer. It came from the very bowels of the world and seemed as old as time. I was pondering on the music of the spheres, the ineffable humming and droning as the great balls of molten rock and gas hurtled their way through the cosmos, when I emerged from the shade of the eucalyptus grove and discovered that the noise was just a tiny bit louder. I was closer to the source. The golden oriole in the eucalyptus trilled out its fluty call, and then I saw them: two youngish couples, sitting cross-legged in a circle (if four people can be a circle) and blowing with intense concentration into didgeridoos.

One of the players caught a glimpse of me and looked up startled. The music stopped.

'Good morning,' I said as the group lowered the long wooden tubes from their mouths.

'Hello,' answered the tallest one, a man with the look of a rather dapper hippy, with neatly pressed clothes and clipped blond beard. 'I hope you don't mind us camping on your land...'

'Not at all, please feel free. It's not every day we wake to the sound of the didgeridoo.' They moved round to make some room for me in the circle.

I learned that they were wandering didgeridoo teachers from Belgium who had come to ply their rather esoteric trade across Andalucia. This would hardly register as unusual amongst the incomers of the Alpujarras – there's a local flamenco teacher from Denmark and a bloke from Sussex who shears the sheep – but I could imagine difficulties in finding pupils for Flemish didgeridoo lessons in wider Andalucia. Still, I kept such pessimistic predictions to myself and, sitting in the dewy grass beside their van, listened to what they had to say about this ancient instrument.

The didgeridoo is a long stem of gum tree, the inside of which has been gnawed out by termites. You don't make your didgeridoo; you find it. You can decorate it to make it more to your liking, but the boring work has to be done by the termites. Heart of eucalyptus is as hard as steel. It's a very ecological sort of instrument; apart from the noise it makes, it has a pretty minimal impact on the environment.

I had a free lesson, but couldn't even get a whimper out of the thing. If you're good, you should be able to make a continuous moaning sound, pulling air through your nose at the same time as you blow it out through your mouth and down the pipe. There was a part of me that day-dreamed about a life on the road, feckless and fancy-free, hauling my didgeridoo from town to town... but on reflection I decided that the dedication wasn't really there.

Waving goodbye to my teachers I headed back up to the house for breakfast. I had a phone call to make.

It didn't take long before we started to lose the romance of making phone calls. There weren't many people we needed to phone and we soon ran out of things to say to those we did. Receiving calls, however, had an air of unpredict-ability about it and therefore kept its excitement. On many an evening we would sit around casting sideways looks at the telephone willing it to ring, but more often than not it didn't.

The first people to start using it were the shepherds; it was getting near shearing time. Before the advent of our telephone, shepherds who wanted me to shear their flocks would actually arrive on our doorstep, more often than not either on muleback or on foot. Others prevailed upon more modern friends with vans to drive them, but even so it was quite an endeavour, as El Valero is a long way down from the mountains where most of the shepherds keep their sheep.

These days Alpujarran shepherds have become pretty adept in the use of mobile phones, but this wasn't the case when our phone was first installed. In those distant days, grappling with a telephone was considered a serious business, and was certainly not to be undertaken when sober.

Typically a shepherd would wait until he had shut his flock in and done all the ancillary jobs before heading for the village and a bar with the necessary apparatus for making a telephone call. The flock would take a dim view of being shut in too long before nightfall; the jobs around the stable would take a good half an hour; the ride or walk to the village could be anything from one to three hours, and upon arrival at the bar, the shepherd would feel the need to fortify himself at length before embarking on the unfamiliar and alarming task at hand. So the early calls would start coming in round about midnight.

When we picked up the receiver, the first thing we would hear would be the music and shouting of a bar, with perhaps the electronic burbling of the fruit machines. There would be a long silence from the other end.

'It's a shearing job,' Ana would say, handing me the phone.

I could imagine the character on the other end holding the handpiece at arm's length, glaring at it with distaste and then shouting loudly at it. Of course when it spoke to them, they couldn't possibly hear, because of the great distance between the diaphragm and the ear, and also the bedlam of noise around them in the bar. So the shepherd would shout at it angrily to speak up.

'CRISTÓBAL!' I would hear as a faint and raucous bellow.

'Yes, speak to me...'

'CRISTOOOBAAL!'

'Alright, I can hear you. Speak now...'

'CRIISTOOOBAAAL!!!'

'YEES! WHAT DO YOU WANT?'

A silence from the other end, as the shepherd digested the idea that the plastic thing with the wire he was shouting at, had actually shouted back at him.

'CRISTÓBAL. WHEN ARE YOU COMING TO SHEAR MY SHEEP?'

'WHO ARE YOU?'

'CRISTOOBAAL!'

'YES, I CAN HEAR YOU, BUT I NEED TO KNOW WHO YOU ARE.'

This would produce a silence on the other end, then some muttering as the other incumbents of the bar were consulted and some advice offered.

'CRISTÓBAL...'

'Look, I need to...' but it was no good, my interlocutor had had enough and slammed the phone down.

That was the way it was with the shepherds on the telephone, though little by little, as they became more adept with it, and picked up a few of the necessary social skills, things got better, until finally we got to a point where we could even exchange rudimentary pieces of information over the phone.

Mistakes however remained inevitable. There was one evening, when Chloë answered the phone quite late at night. I noticed her move the earpiece sharply away from her ear to avoid being deafened by the raucous shout from the other end. 'NO,' she shouted back at the handset, 'YOU CAN'T SPEAK TO MY HUSBAND BECAUSE I HAVEN'T GOT ONE. I'M ONLY SEVEN YEARS OLD!' And she slammed the phone down.

I couldn't help but feel proud of my daughter showing a bit of spirit.

And then, late one evening, the phone rang again. I picked it up and girded myself ready for the deafening shout.

'Chris,' it said softly. 'Is that you?'

It was a person who knew the telephone, a blessing indeed.

'Boss!' I cried. 'Tell me, what news from the wider world?'

'Well,' said Nat, my editor in London, for it was she. 'Are you sitting down? Because I've got some news for you.'

'No, I can't sit down; I'm wedged into the corner by the telephone. That's the way it is here. But I'll lean on something instead.'

'What I'm going to say,' continued Nat in a soft tone, 'is don't get too excited – but *Driving Over Lemons* is going to be read on the radio, and it's being ordered all over the place.'

I stared at the phone. None of us had expected anything like this. It was a bit like entering the local horticultural fete and finding you've won a rosette at the Chelsea Flower Show.

LEAF OF THE MALE

'THERE'S A MAN ON THE TELEPHONE,' said Ana. 'I think he's called Leaf of the Male. He says he wants to speak to you.' 'Seems an odd sort of name,' I muttered, and we both looked at the telephone as if it might hold some sort of clue. But by the time I picked up the receiver, the line was dead. Then of course it dawned on me. It was the journalist – Leith of the *Mail on Sunday*. My book had just been published in England and, to Ana's particular disbelief, had not disappeared without trace. In fact, on the back of a couple of nice reviews, and the reading on Radio Four, it had been charging up into the non-fiction book charts.

It was then that Leith had phoned up and said he wanted to do a story – and he'd be coming out to talk to us at our home in Spain. 'I'll just get a car at Malaga,' he had said, blithely dismissing my attempts to warn him of the perils in store. 'And I'll see you very soon.'

'He probably thinks he knows where we live because of that map in the front of the book,' said Ana. 'You know, the one that you drew.'

I began to feel a bit guilty about my handiwork: the drawings of eucalyptus and olive groves, where perhaps a track or turning might have been more descriptive. I hadn't actually considered that anyone would use the map in the book. It had been more of a *Swallows and Amazons* sort of thing.

In the event, Eugene the photographer and his assistant arrived first. They were smooth and hip and had hired a top-of-the-range silver Volvo at the paper's expense to transport them and their equipment to El Valero. They first appeared racing along the rubbly track in a cloud of dust. Then they hurtled down the unspeakable hill to the river and whooshed straight through the ford – a deed normally attempted by only the most robust and high-slung of four-wheel-drivers.

'It's only a bloody hire car,' drawled Eugene. 'I mean, they don't expect you to polish it outside your villa all week, do they?' Eugene seemed a cool character.

I hovered around the car as the photographers humped out their huge bags and boxes, their silver umbrellas and coloured screens, sun-lamps, chargers and tripods. I thought they were from another planet. 'Last week we done Oasis an' next week the Spice Girls,' commented Eugene.

'How nice,' I said, shuffling my toes in the dust.

'Great spread you got here,' said Eugene, tucking into the *chorizo* and ham and olives we brought out to welcome them. 'Wasn't there supposed to be a journo comin' too?' he asked.

'Yes, that would be Leaf of the Male, but he hasn't turned up yet. I think he's lost.'

'Nothin' would surprise me.' Eugene squinted at the sun. 'Right, let's 'ave a beer or two an' then we'll 'ave you all sittin' up there on that terrace.'

The telephone rang. It was Leaf. He was lost. Ana took the call and gave him detailed instructions on how to find the road to the valley.

It was a hot, hot July day and the sun was raging from a clear sky, as it always does in July. Andrew, Eugene's assistant, was setting up a huge bank of floodlights below the terrace.

'What the hell do you want with that lot on a day like this?' I asked.

'These pics 've gotta be good,' asserted Eugene as he added ever more invasive probosces to his camera. 'I don't like natural light; you can't trust it. Your *Mail* reader don't like to see things in a natural light anyway. Can you do something about your 'air, Chris?'

'Not really, no. It's what's called "flyaway hair" I believe, or what's left of it is...'

I mussed it up a bit with my fingers.

'There, how's that?'

'I s'pose it'll 'ave to do. Now look just above the camera and see if you can raise a grin of some sort...'

The telephone went again. Leaf... still lost.

Eugene and Andrew pushed and pulled at Ana and Chloë and me, and contorted us in and out of all sorts of different positions and poses, and shoved us this way and the other as if we were a family of teddy-bears. Then they did the whole thing all over again but with different lenses and filters and umbrellas and screens, and holding different props and leaning against different things, and then eventually they had the three of us all standing and holding hands and jumping up and down in the river – 'Just try and look natural like, you know, I want you in sort of everyday poses.'

We felt like a family of half-wits, and that, when the photo came out later, was exactly what we looked like – muttonheads allowed out for the day from some sort of institution. Still, Eugene and Andrew were fun, and we all had a good laugh out of it – except of course when we were supposed to be laughing for the camera, when we just looked moronic.

Leaf called several more times in the course of the morning, each time a little bit more lost. We all laughed about poor Leaf, who was apparently some sort of a hot-shot reporter.

'Why would the *Mail* want to send us a hot-shot journo? Surely we're not big news?' I wondered.

'They're treating you like a big one,' Eugene reassured us. 'Not perhaps as big as the Spice Girls, but big nonetheless. So they're sending you Leaf.'

William Leith turned up just before lunch. He was hot and just about as flustered and bothered as I've ever seen a man. He had flyaway hair too, and it was drenched in sweat from the walk up the hill, and his glasses were sticky with dust and muck and he was shaking like a... like a leaf. He reeled into the house and slumped into a chair.

'I'm William,' he said huskily, then smacked his dry lips together. 'Any chance of a beer?'

I brought a bottle – one of those small Spanish ones that wouldn't really register if you poured the contents into a pint glass. William sat back in his chair. Eugene and Andrew looked at each other, then at us. We looked quizzically at Andrew and Eugene. Ana gave me a look. William downed his bottle in one, and then, looking up, noticed that some of us – those of us who weren't looking at each other – were looking at him.

'Lord!' he said. 'Any more where that came from?'

He stayed slumped in his chair with the second bottle, looking like some organism that has somehow got into the wrong element – a deep-sea creature in a bingo-hall, for example. We all stared at him, wondering what he was going to say next. Only when he had finished three beers was he able to communicate.

'Lord God! That road! I have never been so terrified in my life! And then that assault course DIY bridge! I thought I would die... honest to God, look at me; I'm still quaking. Where's the bathroom?'

We assumed that the awfulness of Leaf's experience with the road and the bridge might have loosened his bowels, and ushered him hurriedly to the bathroom. But he didn't shut the door, and as we all peered across we could see him going through the potions and lotions in the cupboards and on the shelves, picking each one up, turning it round and reading the directions for use.

'He's a journo,' explained Andrew. 'That's what they do. They can't help it.'

'He'll be in your knicker-drawer in a minute!' sniggered Eugene.

Sure enough, when William had done his stuff in the bathroom, he wandered out and into the bedroom.

'You wanted to be a famous writer,' said Andrew, 'well, this is what it's all about!'

I wasn't altogether sure that I ever had wanted to be a famous writer, but as we settled down to lunch, William recovered from the traumas of his journey and turned out to be excellent company. We all drank a little more wine than was really good for us and then William got his notebook out and the interview began.

He asked us all sorts of questions – good incisive ones that made Ana and I think a bit – and I warmed to him, and started seeing our life as potentially quite an amusing Sunday newspaper article. I told William everything he asked, cutting short only once when Ana shot me a warning look, and happily spun off into a treatise on the merits of organic farming versus agribusiness, which William politely heard out. Then he turned to me and opened a new page of his notebook.

'It says on the back of your book,' he announced, 'that you were one of the founder members of Genesis. Is there any truth in that?'

'Well, yes,' I said, a little sheepishly. 'But it was a hell of a long time ago, and it lasted less than a year, and to be truthful there's not a lot I can remember about it.'

'Then tell me exactly what you do remember about it,' William insisted...

SIR ROBERT FOSSETT'S
CIRCUS

HOPPING HILL   NORTHAMPTON   NN5 6PA
Telephone 0604 53259

FROM GENESIS TO
THE BIG TOP

THE ODD THING – I found myself telling William – is that me and Genesis began with Cliff Richard. At the age of thirteen I had one great ambition in life: I was going to be Cliff. I don't mean that I was just going to imitate the man (who, I should stress, was then still a heathen rocker) but I was actually going to become him. It seemed to me that to be Cliff Richard would give you everything life had got to give. Now thirty-five years or so later, I realise that I may have been mistaken, but the arguments would not have cut any ice with my star-struck teenage self. Still, as luck would have it, reality soon caught up. I couldn't sing – and the dreams were clearly not to be. So I settled instead on a future as Cliff's guitarist, Hank Marvin.

Of course, being Hank Marvin was no steal, either. God, in his wisdom, had thrown a few obstacles in the way by arranging to have me born tone deaf and by giving me the worst fingernails a guitarist could hope to have. And not just that. These nails extended not from the slender fingers of an aesthete, but from the ham-like mitts of a fitter's mate.

These factors might have quashed my musical career early on had it not been for my best mate Duncan. He was a cool friend to have – lively and wild and a little shifty – and he stood apart from the rest of us at the boarding school where my parents had despatched me. While we young degenerates would bicycle off to some pub to drink and smoke, Duncan would stay behind and put in his regular three hours a day of guitar practice. He was a prodigy and in the holidays had lessons with John Williams.

One summer, experimenting together at being fifteen, Duncan and I met a couple of girls whose pursuit kept us occupied for the whole holiday. One of them – a tall, willowy blonde who could knock the breath out of you with one glance and a swish of her waist-length hair – really was called Eve. Her friend was, by contrast, dowdy-looking, with a lank brown fringe that she continually checked for split ends. I can't remember what she was called, though I do recall a rather sweet smile on the rare moments I looked her way. But my attention was entirely taken up with scrambling over Duncan to get the seat beside Eve, or edging him off the dancefloor, or racking my brains for some witty remark that would prompt Eve's gaze in my direction.

We carried on thus for several gruelling weeks, with sometimes Duncan and sometimes myself gaining a fleeting ascendancy, and Eve playing it for all it was worth. And then one day Duncan brought along his guitar to an evening at Eve's house, when her parents had gone up to London. As he played a series of pieces cunningly selected to win the heart of a fifteen-year-old girl, he stared deep into Eve's eyes, and I knew that I had lost.

Eve's friend knew it was time for both of us to go. In a humane gesture that might well have saved my life, she guided me towards the bus stop, chatting away as the sound of Duncan's guitar faded, and when her bus came she made me look her in the eye and promise that I'd cycle straight home. I pedalled slowly through the streets of Haywards Heath, past the bowling alley and along by the Rose and Crown, sobbing into the night drizzle, blankly following the path home, hoping for death. It feels pretty bad when you're fifteen.

Back at school, miraculously still alive, I set about combatting a future of celibacy. I bought an old guitar from Duncan, with the promise of a few lessons thrown in. I fingered it with awe – the most potent weapon of seduction I could imagine – and set about trying to tune it. It was then that I realised I was tone deaf. Music teachers will tell you there is no such thing as 'tone deaf' but there is, and I was it. Not only was I unable to tune the wretched guitar, but I couldn't tell when it was way out of tune. I would blithely stumble through 'House of the Rising Sun' with no idea why corridors were clearing and study doors slamming.

But I stuck with it. Once a week Duncan would tune the guitar for me and I would practice till my fingers cried. My progress was barely perceptible; I would achieve in three months' relentless practice what most players would do in a week. However, by the end of term I had achieved mastery over the chords of E minor and A major and the changes between them. That's not much. There was an ocean of music out there for me to navigate, and I had barely got the boat out of the harbour. Still, I figured that there was a certain seductive pathos to those two chords, and intelligently deployed, who could say what I might not achieve?

The next summer I went on a school trip to Austria to try and learn German. Among our group was a boy called Skinner, an arrogant, spiteful bit of work, who was rich, good looking and could (as we all tried to at the time) sing and strum Beatles songs rather brilliantly. On a long train-ride to Salzburg, Skinner delighted an entire girl's school contingent with his performance, only to dampen the effect by rolling his eyes and sneering pointedly whenever anyone had the temerity to join in.

Sensing I had nothing to lose I waited until I identified from the position of his fingers an A or an E minor, and then plucked and strummed along, making my tentative display seem more like musical shyness than incompetence. Oddly enough it had the desired effect. Margie, the glittering prize from the girl's school contingent, egged me on to ever greater two-chord triumphs, before deciding that proficiency with the plectrum was not the whole story. For the next three years, until she left me for a louche and handsome poet, Margie eclipsed my world.

At my boarding school, Charterhouse, it was obligatory to be a member of the Corps – the boys' army unit – and this involved two afternoons a week, and even the occasional weekend, of the most unmitigated silliness: square-bashing, polishing kit and learning things that were not of the least interest to anyone other than a homicidal half-wit. There were a few ploys, though, by which you could improve your lot. The best was to join the 'Band and Drums', for which you either had to play some sort of brass instrument (and polish it) or bang a drum – an occupation for which my musical talent fitted me well.

I signed up and was issued with a little book of drum music, a pair of hickory sticks and a snare drum – rather pretty with braid ropes and coloured hoops. On those dismal afternoons when the rest of the school stood at attention in the rain, yelled at and insulted by a man known as the 'Quagger', who took the business of playing soldiers very seriously indeed, we drummers would fool around unsupervised in the Drum Room, smoking, joking and doing our paradiddles, rolls, flams and ratamacues.

Once or twice a term we would have to go out and perform the stuff we had supposedly learned. We would emerge from our Drum Room as disgracefully shabby a bunch of boy-soldiers as you could imagine, apart from Osborne the drum-major who strutted his stuff with the twirly batons at the front, and Hopkins the Welsh oaf who banged the big bass drum. These characters had all the pomp and menace of a two-man Orange Day March but fortunately they were outnumbered. The rest of us would shuffle about sniggering and smirking as the Quagger got more and more apoplectic. We wheeled left when we should have wheeled right; we halted when we should have marked time; we dressed right when we should have dressed left; and we did it all convulsed with suppressed laughter.

Still, the result of it all was that I learned to play the drums. It became a strange sort of obsession. You carried your sticks everywhere and at mealtimes you'd do it with knives and forks, rattling out marches on the refectory tables. And thus my schoolboy military career led me into Genesis.

A year above me at school was a boy called Gabriel, who played the drums for a jazz band, the League of Gentlemen. He had a big old-fashioned drum kit with floppy leather skins that went 'whomp' when you hit them. In an idle moment or two he showed me how, using the pedals, cymbals and a little syncopation, I could adapt my military drumming skills to jazz.

Jazz drumming hit me hard. I was hooked, straight off, and began to hang around anybody who was playing – there were at least a half dozen bands at school – and jump onto the stool as soon as they got off. I got in such a state about it that I would feel sick at the sight of a drum kit. I dropped the guitar completely in favour of my new obsession and practised day and night.

My mentor Gabriel, meanwhile, had begun to sing and play flute with his group. For the flute bits, at least, he needed his hands free, so he asked me to take over the drums. It was an invitation to enter Paradise and of course I jumped at it. We played soul and R'n'B, which was what Gabriel loved most: "When a Man Loves a Woman", "Knock on Wood", "Dancing in the Street" – Otis Redding, Percy Sledge, Wilson Pickett. We played at school functions and at parties in the holidays, and somehow or other got a reputation as the best group in the school. We used to take occasional melodies from the hymnbook, which was perhaps why, along the way, Gabriel re-named us Genesis.

And that would probably have been it, if the enterprising Gabriel hadn't sent a tape to Jonathan King – a maverick who had been at the school a few years earlier, and had notched up a number one pop hit with an awful song called "Everyone's Gone to the Moon". Realising, shrewdly, that he was no popstar, King had begun to forge a reputation as a music producer. He listened to the Genesis tape and, for some reason no one to this day seems able to fathom, decided there was something in our songs of adolescent whimsy that might just propel us into the charts.

King arranged a recording session at an eggbox-lined studio off Tottenham Court Road and the group of us trooped up to London in a state of disbelief, to record three or four of our numbers. They were not the most obvious pop hits – nor, to be honest, very good – but a single was released featuring the most memorable song, "Silent Sun". It sold about a hundred copies. It looked like being a while before we would rival Cliff.

Genesis, however, were a committed bunch, and pressed on with the music business. But my own role in their story was nearly over. I pouted for a few publicity shots and then, at the insistence of my parents, returned to school. The others, whose parents took a more liberal view of pop music as a choice of career, left and set about making an album. They needed a grown-up drummer, so I was given the boot.

It was a good decision on their part – I wasn't really much of a drummer – and I was never going to become Phil Collins. But at the time I was distraught. It felt almost as bad as missing out on Eve. But then Peter Gabriel showed up with a cheque for the startling sum of £300. Apparently Jonathan King wanted everything neat and tidy, and signing a piece of paper would clear up the question of any future rights in the recordings.

I could hardly believe my luck. This was a lot of money.

The following year I left school – with just the one exam pass for Art. No obvious career beckoned so I decided I might as well have another go at becoming a professional drummer. I took some drumming lessons and put an advert in *Melody Maker*, the musicians' paper. It ran as follows: 'Gentleman, 18, seeks position as drummer.'

As I expected from such eccentric wording, I got eccentric replies. One came from a Glenn Miller Big Band that played in the Hare and Hounds in Brighton on Thursday nights – a 'rehearsal and drinking band' they called it. I sat in with them a few times and got very drunk. The other (there were only two) came from Sir Robert Fossett's Circus, which made its living touring the Midlands and north of Britain.

I was interviewed and given the position by Henry Harris, a rather old and classically sad-looking clown, who lived at a caravan site outside Brighton when he wasn't on the road. A part of Henry's act was to galumph around the ring playing "My Blue Heaven" on the trumpet while smoke poured from all those orifices not directly involved with blowing the instrument.

The other member of the circus orchestra was a precise, neatly groomed man called Ken Baker. Half-Polish and rather effeminate, he had the sort of delicate hands I would have liked for my guitar playing, and played that abomination amongst musical instruments, the electric organ. 'I'm so pleased to meet you, Chris,' he enthused at our first meeting. 'I'm sure we're going to make an absolutely marvellous team.'

We opened the 1972 summer season at Queens Hall in Leeds. Ken and I sat in a box on high wheels, wearing red sequinned jackets and bow-ties. We had run through a couple of rehearsals before the show, with Ken playing the tunes and me thumping away alongside. 'Just add a few rolls for suspense,' said Henry the Clown, 'and you'll be just fine.'

But Henry had neglected to mention that Ken had a problem, and a big one for a circus organist – he couldn't busk a note and had to read everything he played. Now in a circus you tend not to play a whole song. What you do is play something stirring and lively while the artiste enters the ring; then something atmospheric while they do their stuff; then, as the acts run their course, you mix the songs up, with the odd heart-stopping silence, before a crisp crescendo drum-roll and crash of cymbals as the artiste flops into the safety net or flings the last knife. Then comes a finale as your artiste sashays out of the ring.

It's not as easy as it sounds, for the organist, at least. There may be snatches of up to a dozen songs in a long act – audiences would get bored with an uninterrupted 'Nellie the Elephant' while Nellie ambled disconsolately around the ring, knelt down, got up, stood on a tub, etc – and each snatch has to be synchronised with the actions. Ken couldn't see the artiste because his head was buried in the music. He had a great sheaf of papers on top of his organ and for each new snatch of song he had to fish out the piece, put it on the music-stand, pull his cuffs up, and strike in. So a crucial part of my role was to relay information to Ken about what was going on in the ring. And with the crashing of the drums, the roaring of the organ, the bellowing of the crowd, and the caterwauling of André the ringmaster, it was often impossible to make him hear.

That first performance, our musical act began to come badly undone during Serena Barontoni's trapeze extravaganza. Serena was a distant member of the Fossett clan, and with her brother Rocco, she did a rather lack-lustre juggling act which consisted mainly of the two of them padding morosely round the ring tripping over the heaps of dropped skittles, batons and brands. But Serena fared better on her own on the trapeze. Her act was not a thing you'd go a long way to see, but it was halfway competent – and it must take a lot more courage to prance about on the ropes and bars at the apex of a big top if you're a mediocre acrobat than if you're a virtuoso.

Serena came on after Zelda, a circus beauty with jet-black hair drawn tightly into a pony-tail, who did ballet-steps standing on the back of one or more horses as they cantered round the ring. All the little girls ooh-ed and aah-ed and formed desperate resolves about their future careers as she sped round and round the ring raising and lowering her perfectly-sculpted legs. She made her exit to "The Magnificent Seven" if I remember right.

'Okay, Ken,' I hissed. 'Zelda's gone – it's André. Then Serena next – "Brazil".'

'Ladeeez ad Jedderbed', howled André. 'De idercweddibawl, luverlee ad glabberuz... Biss Serreeedaaaa BARODTODI!'

'Here she comes, Ken... KEN!..."Brazil"!'

Serena strode into the ring with a look of fierce determination, set above a rictus of a grin. Silence reigned. She swivelled around giving more of the audience the benefit of her simultaneous smile and scowl. The silence continued.

'Ken, she's in – "BRAZIL"!!'

'Alright, Chris, alright!' Ken was getting tetchy. The music had slipped sideways and he couldn't read it sideways. At last the opening chords of "Brazil" blasted shakily out from the organ, but it was too late. Serena had arranged the rope about her person and, with a black look at the orchestra box, started to climb up it as gracefully as her muscular frame would allow. '"Fly Me to the Moon", Ken – for Pete's sake, man!'

Ken was still blithely playing "Brazil". With Serena halfway up the rope, the tune lurched to a halt and Ken started fumbling about. A long silence, then he started into "Fly Me To The Moon". Again it was too late. Serena, now a small glittering figure high up on the flimsy trapezes, was summoning her nerve for a swing into the void. This called for an eerie silence broken by a long crisp drum-roll to build the tension and the terror. *RrrrrrRRRRRRRR B-BOSH!!!* But the tension was somewhat spoilt by "Fly Me to the Moon" trailing after the drum crescendo.

'Right Ken, she's into the swing. Give it all you've got, "Sabre Dance"!!' At this point I would leave the organ and follow the swings and drops and tumbles of Serena's act: *BRRRR-BOSH, BIDDLER BIDDLER-BIDDLER BOSH, BOSHBOSH, BIDDLER-BOSH, BOSH-BOSH-BIDDLER... ting ting titing.* Meanwhile, "Fly Me To The Moon" chundered on, before a silence and then the first hesitant notes of "Sabre Dance" croaked from Ken's organ, as poor Serena hurtled to and fro amongst the hoops and bars at the top of the tent.

At last the wretched act drew to a close and Serena took the rope to return slowly to the sawdust: "There's No Business Like Show Business" came limping from the organ.

'No, Ken, for Chrissakes! She's still up there – it's "Fly Me To The Moon", again.'

'Oh, I'm sorry, Chris – where's that got to now?' and he delved again deep into the mass of music that shrouded his organ. Serena slithered on down the rope in silence, with only the scrunching of crisp packets, chattering of small children and the distant grumble of the generator as accompaniment. 'Mummy, why is that lady so cross?' rang out a toddler's voice from the front row. The answer was drowned by Ken bursting into a desperate repetition of "Fly Me To The Moon". It was too late. Serena flounced from the ring.

'Forget it Ken, she's off.' But no – Ken had to plod his way regardless all the way through "No Business Like Show Business", drowning out André's next 'Ladeez ad Jedderbed...'

'I'm so sorry, Chris,' said Ken afterwards.

I melted. 'Don't worry, Ken, it'll get better with practice...' But of course it didn't. It happened daily, twice on Saturdays, and as the weeks went by I found myself in constant confrontation with poor Ken. On one occasion I even hurled a drumstick at him during a show, an incident provoked by Ken dropping a whole heap of papers on the floor in the middle of an act by the Flying Manzini Brothers, a troupe of volatile and I thought potentially homicidal Italian acrobats.

The Brothers were whizzing round the ring, about a dozen of them piled four high on a one-wheeled bicycle, when, all of a sudden, the music stopped. A muffled oath from the orchestra box, the silly sound of the drums clattering on alone, then round whizzed the Flying Manzini Brothers in silence. Round they whizzed again, cool as cucumbers but mentally hurling knives at the box. Once more they whizzed round. I'm no clairvoyant but I had this strange sense that both Ken and I should avoid walking in the dark behind the tent, especially in the area behind the generator truck where shouts are rather easily masked.

The Fossett Circus travelled all round the north of England and well into Scotland; Leeds, Halifax, Rochdale, Liverpool, Wallasey, Preston, Carlisle, Glasgow, Kilmarnock. I got to know the public bathhouses with their tiled cubicles, enormous baths and polished brass taps gleaming like the controls of ancient steamships, and was initiated into the particular pubs that circus folk frequent. But what I most remember were the long hauls through the dawn of Sunday mornings, after we had packed up the tent at the end of the second show on Saturday night.

Taking down, travelling and setting up the circus was like a battle. As soon as the public started filing out on a Saturday night, you could feel a sudden slackness in the tent as the guy-ropes all around were loosened off and the tent-boys started knocking the six-foot iron pegs out of the ground. The tent-boys, a motley crowd of desperados and runaways, were the lowest of the low in the circus hierarchy – but everyone, even the top artistes, lent a hand to strike the tent and pack up.

It took a couple of hours to drop the big top, which was then folded into impossibly heavy and unwieldy rolls of canvas and loaded with its massive poles onto the trailers.

The circus beasts – which back then featured lions and tigers, elephants, a poor old camel, a llama and a pair of ostriches – were stuffed into their trailers ready for the road. All the seats and the booths and the duck-boards and the poles and guy ropes and flags, the fencing and cables, the lights, the ring, the ropes and bars and hoops and trapezes, the ladders and winches had to be loaded up and lashed down in their appropriate trailers. This was all done in the middle of the night, more often than not in driving rain.

By three or four in the morning everything would be packed and stowed, the trailers hitched to the tugs and the convoy ready to leave. Now was an hour to drink tea and soup, all quiet but for the thundering of the huge generator that ran the lights. Then at last the generator would stop and the remains of the camp sink into a blessed silence. We would climb into the cabs of whatever vehicle we were allotted – I drove the meat-van – and rumble out through the park gates.

We were circus-folk, and this was one of the bits of it that I liked best, crawling in sheeting mists of rain through the few hours that remained of the night, listening to the thunder and whine of the huge road-machines, the ceaseless slapping of the wipers. The headlights picked out the roadsign through the rain: Kilmarnock 50. At our rate of progress that was four hours and more. Drunk with sleeplessness, slumped in the cabs, we were the circus coming to town.

And thus a happy summer passed. I suppose if I'd stuck with it and done a lot of practice on those rolls, then I could have made a pretty good circus drummer, made a career out of it. But it was time to move on and try something else. In Carlisle we set up in a park between the castle and the river and the sun shone all week. One morning I went into town to go shopping, my £20-a-week musician's wage weighing heavy in my pocket, and wandered into a record shop to browse along the shelves. Eventually I decided on a flamenco album.

I can't remember what it was that nudged my destiny in this curious way; I had never heard flamenco and I knew nothing about Spain. But that afternoon, back in my cubbyhole in the accommodation trailer, I got out my little battery-operated record player, stretched out on my foam mattress and played my new record. The guitar was just dazzling. I had no idea you could do things like that with a guitar, or indeed that fingers could ever get so fast. I wasn't altogether sure about the music, but the technique – those fast tripping runs, the deep dark chords and the machine-gun-like percussive effects – sent me reeling.

Suddenly my little repertoire of Dylan and Donovan songs seemed pathetic. I would have to go to Seville and become a real guitarist.

SPANISH GUITAR

I KNEW ALMOST NOTHING ABOUT SPAIN beyond that flamenco record. I certainly spoke no Spanish. But the idea of learning Spanish guitar became an obsession, almost as much as my first schoolboy affair with the instrument, and, bidding farewell to the circus folk, I set off for France to work on the grape harvest and gather money for a stay in Andalucia. From Bordeaux I made my way down to pick oranges in Valencia, where I finally took the Seville bus, which in those days took twelve hours.

I stacked my guitar in the overhead rack and settled back with a shoulderbag stuffed full of oranges. As the bus turned to the west, the last rays of sun shone red and low, making silhouettes of the driver and passengers. I looked in wonder at the palm trees and ranges of dry hills. I had never been this far south before. But as darkness fell, and there was more of me than the view in the glass, I sank into that hazy stupor that a long bus journey induces, dreaming of what might await in Seville.

Spanish buses were different in those days: they rattled and belched and you could open the windows, not that you would have wanted to on a night like that. It was cold outside the bus and the country beyond seemed a little threatening as we climbed inland towards Granada. The bus became my world and I began to dread the idea of leaving it. However, the decrepit old bus rumbled on through the night until at last we turned to follow the Guadalquivir valley and a constellation of lights appeared on the horizon. 'Sevilla,' growled the old man next to me, as the great city unfolded in a vision of industrial yards and slums.

For months I had been longing to arrive in this city but now the real thing was before me, I would have given a lot to be somewhere else. At last, though, we burst through the crust of the suburbs and rumbled along a broad avenue lined with palms and gardens, stone fountains playing at the intersections; and through the stone arch of the Sevilla bus station. I tore myself from the bus and as I stood wondering what to do and where to go, an old man sidled up and whispered conspiratorially: 'Hotel, very cheap.' I followed him, not least because he had my bag.

My guide hurried, wheezing, across a park before ducking into a narrow cobbled alley. The air was a heady mix of jasmine and urine, and a cloud of white moths fluttered around a streetlamp. Our footsteps echoed through the alleys as we turned the bends of a maze and found ourselves in a tiny square, in one corner of which stood a narrow, three-storey house. We entered in darkness. A fat man in a grey suit and dark glasses oiled up out of the gloom: '125 pesetas a night, or 175 full board, cold water only.'

That sounded about right to me, so, with my old man wheezing, and the fat man puffing, and me carrying the bags, we climbed the stairs to the roof and my room. It was a whitewashed brick box with two beds and a chair and a couple of hooks on the door.

I sank into the creaking bed and looked happily at the bare lightbulb. Here I was at last, established in Sevilla. Tomorrow morning I would step out and see the city.

I was too excited to sleep much but must have dropped off eventually for in the morning there entered my dreams the sound of heavy steel poles being dropped on a stone floor. A tiny barred window illuminated my cell, casting a little patch of sunshine high on the wall. The steel poles fell thicker and faster until all the air around was ringing with the sound. I hauled myself up over the rim of sleep and wondered, in that vacuous way before your mind switches on, where on earth I could possibly be and what the infernal noise was?

As I pulled my clothes on and stepped outside, I was almost blinded by the brightness of the morning light. All around were brilliant white rooftops, towers and walls; the sky was powder blue and my own rooftop was a maze of clothes lines and crisp washing. And then the steel poles revealed themselves, too – as churchbells; up here at belfry level, they were close and harsh.

After a breakfast of coffee and toast smeared with raw garlic, olive oil and *sobresada* – that orange butter made from pig fat much appreciated in Andalucia – I stepped tentatively out into the little square, followed a cobbled alley hung with geraniums, and went to seek Sevilla. I passed into a slightly bigger square with four orange trees and a fountain surmounted by three iron crosses. It was perfect. Along another alley scented with jasmine and into another square, more elements were brought into play: some ochre in the white facades, a flower-filled courtyard and a long pool beneath the orange trees.

I strolled, on one whim after another, up and down the alleys. They had names like Water, Air, Jasmine, Life, and each gave onto a *plazuela*, a little square, each more exquisite and lovely than the last. Swooning with a surfeit of beauty, I found myself standing before the colossus of the Cathedral and the Giralda, the great Moorish minaret that the Christians hung with bells.

This glorious urban landscape was peopled by women, and men, more beautiful than I had ever dared imagine, and there was music all around: the sound of a guitar or piano practised behind an open balcony door, snatches of singing and clapping on the warm city air. The smells were strong, too: coffee, black tobacco smoke, garlic, the exhausts of mopeds, *Heno de Pravia*, the sweet cologne so many Spaniards use, and everywhere the scent of the thousands of orange trees.

I walked around the city all day in a daze, missed lunch, and forgot that my feet were sore. Then as the evening cool took hold, I found my way back to the hotel square – Mezquita, it was called – in time for a supper of lumps of pig fat swimming in a lake of beans and cloves of boiled garlic, with wine, bread and an orange to round it off. It was ambrosia.

The next morning I did some washing in a stone basin on the roof. It was pleasant slopping water about in the

December morning sunshine. As I was ineptly scrubbing away, whistling a tune to myself, a figure emerged from the companionway that connected the roof to the rest of the hotel. She was a well-built woman in her forties, wearing high heels, a tight pencil skirt and a man's white vest, and she looked at me in amazement.

'What on earth are you doing?' she asked.

'Washing. I'm doing my washing,' I answered, rather pleased with myself. I'd discovered on my journey south that this was an inevitable question and that if I so much as dunked a grey undergarment under some suds, someone, somewhere, was sure to pop up and ask it. With a bit of foresight I'd worked out the answer from my dictionary. My Spanish was pretty rudimentary but still my companion managed to get the idea across that I was to cease immediately because it wasn't seemly for a man to wash his own clothes, and that henceforth she would do it for me. She took over straight away, and while she splashed about, I attempted to reciprocate by serenading her on the guitar. Even in my guitar-besotted state I couldn't quite convince myself that the deal was entirely fair.

My new friend was called Isa. She worked at the hotel and seemed to take something of a shine to me. Sometimes in the evenings, she would take me out to a bar with her younger friend Viki, who was plump and rather pretty and giggled a lot. They would take a lot of trouble dressing up for these occasions, emerging from their rooms in staggeringly high heels, fishnet stockings, deep-cleft cleavages and a few pots of lavishly-daubed make-up. The pair of them would look me over and pick hairs and crumbs and what-have-you off my crumpled shirt, and straighten my hair before declaring us ready. Then off we'd go, clacking and hobbling through the cobbled streets to some lowish sort of a bar.

It was kind of Isa and Viki to take me on these expeditions, I always thought, as I couldn't have been very much fun for them. The three of us would lean on the bar, where my companions would get maximum effect from their stockings and split miniskirts. They would gabble together, occasionally turning to shoot me a good-natured grin. I would grin back politely and return to grappling with the language.

I wanted very much to join in their conversation, and kept working out things I could say to them with the aid of a pen and paper and a Spanish dictionary. But of course, by the time I had constructed a suitable conversational gambit, the moment had always passed, and I would be reduced to the sheepish grin.

Still, I took a lot of pleasure from these evenings, and from the Mezquita generally. It was a noisy but friendly sort of place, whose other residents were mostly young men from the country, working in a factory just across the river. At our evening meals we would engage in a stilted inter-course of half-sentences, baffled grins and raised eyebrows. But, odd though it may seem, I must have been a social asset, for they too took me to bars.

On one such outing, I found myself in a grotto-like bar full of students and smoke and lively chatter, when in strode a huge woman with such a powerful presence that the babble was suddenly silent. At her heels followed a tiny boy with a guitar-case bigger than himself. One of my companions dug me in the ribs and smirked. 'Fat Lola,' he said, and he indicated with his hands – rather unnecessarily – her shape.

Fat Lola took a seat against the wall and a space was cleared before her. She took the light, yellow guitar from its case, and holding it almost at arm's length among the folds of her great body, she sent her fingers wandering powerfully and easily across the strings. Some slight adjustment to the pegs and away she went. There was a reverential hush. Sharp arpeggios jangled from the strings. Her improvisation soared and swooped, moaned and wailed, and then rose to a roar as she beat at the instrument with the fastest, most flexible wrist I ever saw. I had never heard live flamenco guitar, and I was spellbound. The unfamiliar oriental ring filled the music with mystery and anguish, and the ease and power of her playing made it seem as if the guitar were playing itself.

The song sank to a low repetitive moan, like a challenge repeated. One of the factory workers stepped into the space and knelt before Lola on the floor. Cries of '*Olé!*' and '*Anda!*' rose from the audience. The guitar coaxed and cajoled him, teasing the song from him, then all of a sudden he cried out as if in great pain. The cry became a wail and a deep moan, culminating in a long strained ululation. As he worked his way through couplet after couplet, he wept real tears. I was utterly transfixed.

The next day I set out in search of a guitar teacher. I didn't have to look far. Breakfasting on coffee and doughnuts in a bar, I found Xernon sitting next to me, a blond, chubby-faced boy, half-Mexican, half-American. He looked about twelve years old but he had a guitar-case with him and we got talking. 'If you want to learn flamenco,' he told me, 'then you must stay at the Hostal Monreal; that's where everyone stays. I'll take you there if you want.'

So I left my friends at the Mezquita – Xernon had been surprised to find I was staying at a brothel (as even I had begun to suspect after a few nights out with Isa and Viki) – and, swinging my guitar, walked to the Cathedral, where the Hostal Monreal stood on the corner. I gave my details at the desk to a woman called Mary, a pretty, soft-spoken Irishwoman who did the books, kept the staff happy and mediated with the rag-bag assortment of guests, most of them guitar students or dancers.

Mary's lover, José, was the owner of the place. He was to be seen at all times of day or night hovering about with a pipe-wrench and a deeply worried look on his face. He liked to fix the plumbing and his dream was to get rid of the scruffy clientele and fill his hotel with rich American tourists. Had he made a better job of the plumbing, he could probably have raised the paltry 175 pesetas he charged for 'full board, cold water only.'

But the plumbing was in a class all of its own. To get the full benefit of the cold shower you had to lean against the tiles beneath the hole where the water dribbled out of the wall, and then by contorting your neck and shoulders you could guide the trickle to whatever part of your body required it. It was not the sort of thing calculated to arouse the enthusiasm of big-spending Americans.

The Monreal had three floors with wooden balustrades overlooking a central patio with battered aspidistras and a dribbling fountain illuminated by green and red fairy-lights.

On the flat roof were washing lines and two roof-huts, which were a little cheaper than the proper rooms. They were ovens in the daytime, while at night you needed a hundredweight of bedclothes to keep your teeth from chattering. I took one of these for a month and set about my mission.

The guitarists at the Monreal were an international bunch and most of us were in our late teens or early twenties. Occasionally, however, a more experienced player would drift through to reminisce, do a bit of teaching or patronise us rank beginners by joining a session. Herb was the exception. A wiry American with a pony-tail sprouting beneath an incipient bald patch, he puzzled us all by managing to combine extreme old age (he was thirty-one) with a ham-fisted incompetence. I remember pondering in amazement his decision to take up guitar in the twilight of his life, and in the fog of youth I even asked him once: 'I mean, hell, man, why bother!' It was a phrase that would come back to haunt me.

Practice sessions were held daily on the roof and the keener among us would sit up there playing for eight to ten hours a day. Of course it was the most beastly sound, with everyone running up and down different scales and loosening their wrists with noisy *rasgueados*, all on very loud, strident guitars. You couldn't see the faces of the players, as they were hidden by washing; all you could see were the chairs, the trousers and guitars, though if you leant back you could look up through the sheets to the towers and balconies of the city, and the deep blue sky. Every now and then one of the chambermaids would come up and, under the guise of checking the washing, indulge in a little flirtation.

One day, drinking together in a respite from the guitars, we all agreed that our rehearsal studio really was intolerable, and came up with some rules to make practice more fruitful. From then on, anybody who wanted to practise on the roof had to play with a sock stufffed under the strings until midday, and no player was to drink or offer wine before lunchtime.

And so the routine was established. We would sit out the morning, feverishly blipping at our guitars until the bell tolled, when the socks were whipped out, bottles of wine produced, and the free ringing of seventy-two strings would begin again. Sometimes the routine would be broken by the arrival of an old man with a Cordobés hat, who had been teaching one of the more advanced players in his room. Then we would all listen spellbound as he tripped through a series of *falsetas*, dazzling us with his technique.

Winter passed, and with the arrival of the first months of spring, white stars began to appear amongst the dark leaves of the orange trees and the first heat of the year began in earnest. In Tokyo and Los Angeles, temperature inversions create clouds of smog that hang for days over the city, choking people to death. In Sevilla, which is the most romantic city in the world, the heavy cloud of orange-blossom scent that envelops it in spring and early summer drives people mad with love.

At the Monreal, the object of all our madness was Laura, an American who was learning to dance flamenco. She had curly chestnut-coloured hair, a turned-up nose and wide hazel eyes, and moved with the graceful swish of bamboo leaves in the wind. Everybody was crazy about her, but moving ethereally among the musicians she seemed to have no inkling of the effect she was having upon us.

The air at the Monreal thickened with sexual rivalry and we rushed into combat with our guitars. The poor girl must have had little sleep for our interminable serenading, while during the day hopeful accompanists would line up to offer their services for her dance practice. Alas, I wasn't even in the running for this honour, being easily outgunned by Xernon and the rest of the group's virtuosos.

It was an all too familiar tale but again it advanced my musical skills. One night I had been practising with Paul, a fellow student, down in the Maria Luisa park, when he began playing a light classical piece called "Romanza". I listened with rapt attention. The tune was indeed romantic, utterly so, and touched with a deep poignancy, but most of all it was simple. I thought if Paul could give me a bit of coaching, I might soon get the hang of it and be in with a chance at last with Laura. Paul, who was gay and thus out of the chase, said he'd be happy to help.

It wasn't quite as easy to learn as I'd imagined but eventually I mastered the piece and had only to wait for an opportunity to perform it. None came. Each time Laura appeared on the roof one of my betters would muscle their way to the fore with some fiery flamenco piece and monopolise her for the rest of the practice. Meanwhile, I'd pick away at my "Romanza" with a dreamy expression on my face, from my stool behind the washing, with the likes of old man Herb drowning out my finer moments.

I decided to take action. One afternoon when Laura had disappeared into her room, I followed and knocked timidly on her door. She opened it with a not entirely impatient look of enquiry on her face. 'I'd like to play you a tune,'

I blurted. 'I think it might help you to relax after all that dancing.'

There was a pause. Laura smiled, a sad, slightly off-centre smile and replied. 'Okay, but promise me it's not that piece you've been playing all week on the roof. I really could not bear to hear you crucify that again... I mean, not right up close.' And then she added, puzzlingly, 'You see, that movie was just *so* beautiful and *so* upsetting and *so*, like, true, that I want to keep it fresh in my mind.' Laura was clearly one of those people who believed in being cruel to be kind – an odd notion because I imagine most people prefer their kindness unalloyed.

'Yup, of course, no problem... that's fine,' I managed to mumble as I backed off down the corridor. But even without the humiliation ringing in my ears, Laura's comments had stumped me. What on earth was all that about a movie?

Xernon passed me. He was struggling to hold back a smirk, then, realising I was genuinely in the dark, he stopped to elucidate. 'You've been playing the theme tune from that French film, *Les Jeux Interdits*, you dork, didn't you know?' I still looked blank. 'You know, that old black and white movie that has been showing down at Plaza Nueva?' I shook my head. 'About a poor orphan girl and her dead dog in occupied France?'

Finally the smirk broke free, spreading across Xernon's face like a rash. 'Not exactly flamenco,' he commented.

Romance at the Monreal was a fine and character-forming thing. But what I had really fallen in love with was Spain. And having done so, what I really wanted to be was Spanish, or what I then imagined Spanish to be: olive-skinned and brown-eyed, a deft hand with a sharp knife and an orange, a natural guitarist, a Don Juan.

As the months went by, I realised that I wasn't going to cut it. My nose went English-red; I tended more to the reflective than the excitable; I was – let's face it – a rotten guitarist; and my skills as a seducer were hampered by a tendency to mental paralysis when faced with the object of my affections. In addition, my money was spent. Sevilla was drawing to a close for me.

As the summer heat became intense, I took a carriage to the station and boarded a night train full of soldiers. The train took me to Barcelona and from there I hitch-hiked to Paris, where I played guitar in the Métro to replenish my funds. There was a long tiled corridor at the Étoile station, where I made my stand. Its acoustics were remarkable, making a quietly-plucked Spanish guitar sound like a full orchestra, and, amongst other things, I played "Romanza". It was a way of exorcising my humiliation and I liked to think the middle section was shaping up nicely. People stopped to listen by the dozen, and seemed to go pensive and a little melancholic before dropping a fat coin in my hat.

It turned out that *Les Jeux Interdits* was playing to full houses at the Étoile cinema. My luck was in. In a short time I had enough money to buy a ticket home to England.

Back under northern skies, my guitar ambitions were gradually replaced by new and rather contradictory passions – farming and travel. My time in Seville had left me hooked on the idea of flinging myself into unknown seas, while a brief stay on a sheep farm in the Black Mountains in Wales and a job on a farm in Sussex gave me a glimpse of a career path without suit and tie. For the next twenty years I farmed, for the most part, with an odd stint helping to research travel guides. The guitar would just occasionally resurface in my life – one winter I got a Saturday night slot playing at a Russian restaurant in Fulham – but it would be nearly twenty years before I found myself back in Spain with time on my hands for another crack at flamenco.

LITERARY LIFE

A COUPLE OF DAYS AFTER LEAF had cautiously picked his way back over our bridge, I had another phone call from London. This time it was my publisher, Nat, calling to say I'd been invited to talk at the Hay Literary Festival. She went on to enumerate the advantages for a writer of appearing at this gathering of book folk on the Welsh borders, but my mind had begun to drift. I was recalling the time when I'd stayed on that hill-farm in the Black Mountains and first learned how to shear sheep.

'Of course I'll come, if they want me,' I enthused at once. 'The countryside around Hay is as nice as it gets, and I could look up some old friends.' Nat seemed relieved and talked on matter-of-factly about what a pleasant break it would be; she and Mark, the other half of my publishers, would drive down and meet me there. Then by way of parting she added that I shouldn't worry at all about reading from or discussing my book – 'just be yourself,' she said, 'and you'll be fine.'

That's when the nostalgic sheep-shearing images evaporated and the realisation dawned that I was to address a literary audience. I turned to Ana and Chloë – perhaps they could come too? But no, it was too short notice and the animals and school would have none of it. So it was that two weeks later, dragging an odd assortment of books in a leather bag (well, I could at least pass muster as a reader), I stepped apprehensively into the ticket and reception area at the Hay-on-Wye festival office.

A light spattering of rain was replenishing the puddles at the centre of the festival courtyard, while slithery duck-boards conducted the literary-minded to various tented auditoria. Nat and Mark were easy to spot, splashing around in the puddles with their toddler, near a door that led into a primary school classroom, transformed for the week into an authors' reception room. I joined them just as a small knot of people paced past and some heads turned.

'That's Vikram Seth, I think,' said Nat. 'He's talking in the tent next to yours – same slot, sadly, so we'll all miss him.' I turned to see the back of one of my favourite authors disappearing into another tent, just as two women swathed in kagouls pointed in my direction, whispering in a loud, excited hush, 'It's him! I'm sure it is!' This was heady stuff. I straightened up and beamed back at them as an arm lightly touched mine to guide me out of the way. 'Thank you,' murmured Bill Bryson in passing.

I don't think I need to try and illuminate the blur that followed, except to say that a sympathetic festival organiser steered me through the door of the primary school classroom, poured me some wine and introduced me to my co-panellists Monty Don, the garden writer, and Adam Nicolson, author and newspaper columnist. I recall doing little more than smiling and gulping, with my eyes fixed on a small cardboard spider that dangled on one side of Adam's head, painted, apparently, by "Megan, aged 6yrs". Before I could ask for another glass, the kindly organiser was ushering us all in and out of the rain again and onto a stage. My publishers and their toddler smiled wanly from some seats next to the tent door. It was the sort of smile that you might use to cheer a relative in the dock.

Adam began talking and reading from his book. I don't think I'd ever longed for someone to be long-winded before – and he didn't oblige. He was pithy and funny and, it had to be said, literary. I picked the dirt from under my nails and waited for my awful exposure, for someone to stand up at the back and say, 'That man's not an Author – he's a sheep-shearer.' Instead Monty Don swung into the gentlest of introductions and asked me to read a passage that he'd marked out. It was a description of my first ever shearing expedition in the Alpujarras, when I'd had to face down the scepticism of the local shepherds about using electric shears.

I looked down at the page and suddenly realised that I hadn't a clue how to read it. It wasn't that my literacy skills had deserted me but I just hadn't any idea what the voices of the different shepherds bantering with each other should sound like in English. At the time we had all spoken in Alpujarran Spanish and in the book I had side-stepped the issue of regional voices by recording their idiosyncratic grammar and leaving their accents to the imagination. Monty looked at me, Adam looked at me. The rain drummed patiently on the roof of the tent as if waiting also. I picked an accent, more or less at random and flung myself on the mercy of the hall.

The first shepherd announced his serious doubts about the safety of his flock in the voice of a Pantomime Pirate, a kind of Ben Gun–Cornish. I coughed and tried again. He was answered by a Somerset lad who had evidently spent a lot of time in the Transvaal. I stopped once more. Out of the corner of my eye I noticed Nat get up and, in a crouching tip-toe, leave with their toddler under her arm. Mark was staring fixedly up at the roof of the tent, seemingly amazed to find that it was made of canvas.

I continued. The first shepherd had settled into an altogether quieter and more manageable Sussex country voice. That was fine, but I – the narrator – had somehow turned into Prince Philip. I ground to an appalled halt.

'I'm sorry,' I started to say, 'I really don't know where all these strange accents have come from.' But my words were obliterated by a ferocious thrumming on the roof of the tent. It seemed that God, in answer to my fervent prayer that the ground should open up and swallow me, had arranged for the skies to open instead. Perhaps he hadn't quite got the hang of my accent.

I leant back, saved by the elements, and watched as Nat swept back into the tent with a sleeping child in her arms. She smiled broadly at me. While the rain continued none of us could do anything more than smile. It was impossible to hear a word that anyone spoke, even if they were next to you. I pictured Vikram Seth, smiling and waiting on the stage of the tent behind and thought what a great leveller rain is.

After the deluge the audience and panel exchanged thoughts in the most relaxed manner imaginable about farming and literature. Then we all wandered out into the brilliant sunshine to a tent where piles of books were waiting to be signed. I couldn't help but notice a herd of cows plodding across their damp field above the festival grounds as if intending to join the queue.

When I returned from this literary trip, which included a few booksignings in local shops as well looking up my old sheep-farming friends, Ana and Chloë checked me closely for signs of uppity-ness. Chloë enjoyed hearing me recount how I had signed books for complete strangers in bookshops but seemed anxious that I might have become changed in some subtle, irreversible way.

I knew what she meant. Interest in authors struck me as being a fleeting, giddy-making thing. The phone rang, and in proof of how suggestible I'd become, I picked it up expecting it to be a journalist pressing for an interview. Instead it was José Guerrero, my shearing partner.

'YOU'RE BACK FROM OVER THERE. GOOD,' he shouted. 'TOMORROW WE'RE GOING SHEEP-SHEAR-ING!'

'No we're not. I've just this minute got home.'

'NO MATTER, THESE SHEEP HAVE GOT TO BE DONE. SEE YOU AT FIVE-THIRTY IN RAMÓN'S BAR.'

'Look, I don't want to go shearing tomorrow; I've already been away and now I want to get to know my family again.'

'I'M COUNTING ON YOU, CRISTÓBAL. YOU CAN GET TO KNOW YOUR FAMILY ON THURSDAY.'

'Why can't you shear them yourself?'

But it was too late; the other end of the line was dead.

Chloë wasn't particularly enthusiastic about my heading straight off shearing, but Ana understood. She knows that I've never been able to refuse José Guerrero any favour.

José is an original. He hides a nature of quiet thoughtfulness and warmth beneath a brash bumptious exterior. A couple of years ago he was diagnosed with cancer of the lymphatic system, which probably explains his curiously cadaverous appearance. His way of coping with the disease is to hurl himself into a life of constant frenzy. To be with him is exhausting; he burns you up with his relentless energy. The technique seems to work, though; the disease seems unable to take the pace, and each time I see him he is just a little better, taking a few less pills.

Both Ana and I felt that a day's grubby manual work with José Guererro might help to bring me back to earth from the rarified realms that I had been inhabiting.

At five o'clock in the morning there's not a stitch of light in the sky, just the stars, and on that particular morning there was no moon. I rolled quietly from the bed and stumbled around trying to find my tee-shirt and jeans, then crept out of the house into the hot, dark morning. Trudging along the track, I strained to catch the sound of the nightingales

singing over the crunch of the gravel and roar of the river.
All around the great bellies of the mountains stood dense
black against the imperceptibly greying sky. The pale yellow
bloom of the *gallomba* lining the track glowed feebly and
the scent of its flowers filled the night. Then I crossed the
bridge, climbed into the car, and, flicking on the headlights,
extinguished the spell of the morning.

In Ramón's the usual early morning suspects sat along
the bar addressing themselves quietly to their coffees,
manzanillas, anis and brandies. There was no sign of José so
I took a stool and ordered an orange juice. A young man in
a shiny tracksuit came in and started cracking jokes about
football in a loud voice. The other members of the bar
seemed to enjoy it, but my thoughts were drifting back to
home and bed. Whatever had made me want to do sheep-
shearing, on a day that the TV weather lady was just saying
would be around thirty-five degrees?

At half past six, José stepped into the bar and slumped
down beside me. 'You're right on time,' he said. 'Good –
let's go.' I knew he had said five-thirty but there seemed
no point in arguing the point. José had overslept but he's a
man who doesn't like to admit mistakes, and to be honest,
he looked a bit rough, and like he didn't need an argument.

I slung my bag into the cramped and fetid cab of José's
van and squeezed in after it. He started the engine and
slipped a tape into the machine. Full volume, hideously
distorted.

'You'll like this, Babykin...' he announced.

'What?'

'*La música* – it's Baby Kin...'

'Ah, you mean BB King?'

'*Si, claro* – I just got this tape. Listen, it's an Elmore James song.'

José is crazy about the blues. Well, so am I, at a decent hour of the day. But José seems to have some sort of short circuit in his sensibility system so that he enjoys it blasted out at full volume even at dawn. Inspired by Babykin's guitar riffs, he thrashed the little tin van mercilessly up the Sierra de Lújar.

It was a hot morning even now, before the sun had risen, and we had both windows open which dispelled a little the miasma of sheepshit and cigarette smoke. As we climbed higher, the snow-capped crests of the Sierra Nevada began to reveal themselves, and beneath them the grey of the high mountains looming above the dim blue folds of the valleys. We wound on and on up the narrow mountain road, through thick banks of deep grass and flowers, over the little pass above Camacho, and headed east along the ridge and up to the highest point along the road, Haza del Lino. Here we stopped at the bar to ask the way.

'Is Blas here?' José asked the dark-eyed beauty behind the bar.

'No, he's up in the Sierra.'

'But he's expecting me today. Didn't he get the message?'

'Mother!' called the girl. A woman fresh from the frying in the kitchen peered round the door at José.

'Ah yes. I didn't give Blas your message because he didn't come home last night.'

'When will he be back?'

'No way of knowing.' The two women looked at one another doubtfully, then at José.

'How do we find him, then?' he asked.

'It's very difficult,' the mother began, with a look that made it seem like it really was very difficult.

'How, then?'

'Well, you go along the road towards Venta de Tarugo... and then you take the first right...'

'No, you're better off going past Tarugo and left,' offered an old man who sat at the bar.

'Manuel, what do you know? It's much quicker going down and then up...'

'Manuel has a point, though...' butted in another customer.

And so it went on, a melee of passionate and apparently contradictory advice, until at last we emerged with a piece of paper marked with what looked like runes, and a self-appointed guide, called Miguelillo, who seemed to have a very sketchy command of local geography. However, he purported to know just where we would find Blas.

Miguelillo got in the front and I stretched out across the back seat and watched the world, or that part of it composed of the Sierra de la Contraviesa, zoom by through the side windows. We turned down to Venta de Tarugo along a lovely little road, with flowers and grasses growing through the tarmac.

We could see the sun now hanging fiercely over the distant Sierra de Gador. Every bend we wound around took us into almost complete blindness, the white light of the sun enhanced by the disgusting state of José's windscreen and the fact that both sun-visors had long ago dropped off. To either side stretched rolling hills of vines, short stocks with long dark shadows cast by the low sun. A few men were out in the vineyards in the early morning cool, one man tiny and alone in a sea of vines, hacking away at the weeds with his mattock – a truly Herculean labour. Nobody lived here. I couldn't imagine even sheep living here. On we went, and on and on. There were few side-turnings, no villages, no houses, nothing but the vines.

Miguelillo looked increasingly bemused and it soon became clear that he scarcely knew who Blas was, let alone where he could be found. He was one of those people, and they are to be found everywhere in rural Spain, who hang around in bars waiting for something interesting to happen – say a ride in a car somewhere. Just in case we were left in any doubt as to his usefulness, he told us he had a psychological disorder that made him violent from time to time. He was alright mostly, but when he got wound up, he just couldn't stop himself. He said it made it difficult for him to hold down a proper job. He told us all this with a smile that would charm your worst aunt.

José, too, was all smiles, as he turned to Miguelillo and addressed him:

'*Hombre,*' he said. 'All this is very bad luck, and me and my friend here count it a great privilege to have you with us as a guide today – even though you haven't the first idea where the hell we are. But I'm just taking this opportunity to let you know that if you step just one tiny little step out of line, we will have no hesitation in hanging you by the balls from one of these cork trees. Cristóbal in the back there now is very quiet and gentle-mannered, but he gets evil when he's riled up, and there's no stopping him. Do you understand what I'm saying?'

Miguelillo understood perfectly and said that he thought it extremely unlikely that he would turn nasty. I just watched the flowers of the roadside racing by outside the side-windows, and hoped that I wouldn't have to get evil.

Not long afterwards, after a couple of wrong turnings and no help at all from Miguelillo, who had decided to get out at a crossroads where there was a big shady fig tree, we happened upon the *cortijo* where we were to do our stuff. In order to try and build up some momentum I flung open the door and leapt out into the warm sunshine of the yard. A line of big dark men in blue boiler suits considered our arrival through a curtain of cigarette smoke, and beneath a walnut tree a couple of thin dogs scratched themselves on bits of rusty agricultural detritus.

'How could anyone want to be anything other than a sheep-shearer?' I exclaimed to José, as we set up the machinery in the barn below.

The day started to unfold in just the way that such days do, the heat increasing and the sweat running and the flies swarming over us. But it didn't bother us at all because the sheep were perfect. They sheared like a hot knife through butter, the wool furling off neat and clean. José, singing to himself, turned on the speed to make a competition of it. I speeded up, too, and all morning we raced through those wonderful fat sheep together. As the day drew on and the sheep heated up and started sweating, it got better still. A hot, fat, sweaty sheep is a shearer's dream. By mid-afternoon we had finished the job, and were down at the house sharing a meal with the shepherd and his family.

Later we loaded the clobber back in the van and headed off down the track. Miguelillo was still sitting beneath his fig tree at the crossroads. José pulled up and looked at him, bathing him in a cloud of cigarette smoke.

'I suppose you want to show us the way back now?'

Miguelillo thought about it a bit, then, seeing me looking at him from the passenger seat, decided against it.

'*Gracias* – but I've got a few things to attend to first. I'll make my own way back.'

A Parrot in the
Pepper Tree

O UTSIDE OUR HOLIDAY COTTAGE, El Duque, is a False Pepper Tree. We planted it as a seed, a little thing encased in what looks like a red peppercorn – but isn't. *Schinus molle* (the Latin name) grows at an astonishing rate. Within three years it had become a full- blown tree with a thick peppery-barked trunk and a great mass of pendulous green foliage set with little clouds of false red peppercorns. You could happily doze and while away the afternoon hours in its shade. It hangs over the cottage gate.

One July morning, as Ana was passing beneath the pepper tree with a sack of washing in her arms, something bright green and feathery fluttered down and landed on her shoulder. It was a parrot – not a bird you see much of in Andalucia. It perched quietly and looked at her, its head on one side, and stayed there as she opened and loaded the boot of the car. 'Hallo,' said Ana, who is not a person to be caught off guard by an event like this. 'Do you want to come home with me, then?'

The parrot shuffled closer to her head and nibbled her ear in what she took to be a friendly way. 'Well, it would be a fine thing to have our very own parrot, but let's go and see if Antonia knows anything about you first,' Ana suggested.

Antonia was the obvious person to ask about parrots because she'd been looking after Yacko, her Dutch family's pet African Grey, for the last couple of years. Yacko is ancient and, as a result of a feather-pecking habit, resembles a small plucked turkey, with a huge beak and one scarlet feather sticking out of its butt. Since moving south he has spent most of his time hiding behind the fridge, from where he surveys a thin sliver of the Alpujarran landscape with a jaundiced eye, pining no doubt for the polders and tulips and the grey skies of home.

When Ana arrived with a stray parrot on her shoulder, Yacko couldn't help but edge his beak around the front of the fridge to take a look. He gave an almightly squawk and scuttled backwards, jamming himself in among the pipes. Yacko does this to people, too, if less dramatically, like a suburban householder retreating behind their net curtains. Later, though, I wondered if Yacko hadn't picked up on some deep and irremediable personality flaw in Ana's windfall parrot.

Antonia had heard nothing about a missing pet but promised to help spread the word around the valley and into town. Meanwhile she loaded Ana up with seeds and useful advice about the bird's diet and general care. The parrot seemed to like the idea of going home with Ana and clung to her shoulder as she climbed into the front seat and started the engine. Then, as the car bounced across the valley to El Valero, it stepped delicately onto the back of the passenger seat, as if to survey its new home.

Over the next fortnight we asked around if anyone had lost a parrot. No one had heard anything and the local consensus was that it was from *la providencia* – heaven sent. That suited us, as we had always wanted a parrot yet had not wanted to support a questionable trade by actually buying one from a pet shop.

Domingo, ever in the know, suggested that our parrot might have been an escapee from the ornithological park of Loro Sexi (named, oddly enough, after a Phoenician admiral), down on the coast. Another engaging theory came from Rachel, who makes exquisite jewellery at her *cortijo* near Orgiva.

'So *you* got the parrot, then,' she said, with an unmistakably accusing edge to her voice.

'What on earth do you mean by that?' I asked.

'Well, if you want a parrot enough, and your energy is right, then a parrot will come. I was after a parrot myself, you see. I felt the time was right for me to have one, so I built a big cage and left the door open, and then started to get the energy up in order for a parrot to come...'

'Rachel, I think you are completely doolally.'

'No, wait, I was out for a walk last Friday – the day you got your parrot, yeah? Well, I was walking in the riverbed concentrating on the particular sort of parrot I wanted to turn up. All of a sudden there was a whoosh of wind and a puff in the dust at my feet. Of course I thought it was my parrot, but when I stooped to pick it up, it was a dead bird, tiny, like a pebble. So you see, it seems you got the parrot and I got the dead bird – it's the story of my life...'

'Look, I'm sorry, Rachel, we didn't mean to take your parrot from you, but I don't think there'd be any possibility of moving it now. It's attached itself to Ana in a big way.'

'Oh no, no, you go ahead. Enjoy your parrot. I'll keep working on the energy and, who knows, maybe next time I'll have better luck.'

In fact our parrot turned out to be not a parrot at all but a Quaker Parakeet and, as far as anyone could tell, a male. Sexing a parrot is not an easy matter, unless you happen to be a parrot, or have access to DNA testing, or catch your bird laying an egg. Telling the difference between parakeets and parrots, by contrast, is straightforward. Parakeets are a good deal smaller, midway between a budgie and a macaw. Our specimen is a luminescent green with a grey under-belly, a big orange beak and beautiful blue tips to his wings and tail.

Initially we called him Lorca, but the great poet's name sat ponderously on the bird – it seemed just too noble for our small feathery interloper. Then, one lunchtime, Ana was watching the parakeet nibbling a lump of ham from Chloë's plate. Ana held up another piece: 'Here, Porca,' she called. There was a flutter of wings as our parrot claimed both his snack and his name.

Porca made himself at home from the very minute he arrived. He surveyed all the dogs and cats from the eminence of Ana's shoulder or the top of her head, and took stock of his new kingdom and its subjects. In a matter of days he had subdued the unrulier elements and established a pecking-order with himself at the top, as a sort of captain's mate to Ana. Below them came an amorphous order of various dogs and cats and Chloë, then, somewhere round about eleven or twelve, me.

It's humiliating but any attempt I make to gain promotion gets firmly rebutted. If I try to pamper him, say by offering up a piece of banana skin (which Porca seems to prefer to the fruit), he will nibble away at it for a while, then show disdain for my attempt to ingratiate myself by pecking me hard on the finger.

Porca lives free and his chosen territory is the bathroom, where he perches all night upon the shower taps, which Ana has covered indulgently with old bog-roll inners for the bird's comfort. From there he launches ferocious attacks on anybody who for whatever reason visits the bathroom.

Porca is particular about not only guests in his bathroom but objects. He detests above all the presence of the blue plastic toothmug on top of the washing-machine cover, so sometimes, to keep my end up, I place it carefully on that very spot. It never fails to enrage him. Incensed, he hurls himself from his shower tap at the offending mug, trying to guide it towards the gaping lavatory to score the longed-for hit and watch the loathed object float on the waters within. He can be further tormented by filling the mug up with water so he can't move it, or shutting the lid of the lavatory. Such are my small revenges on my rival.

During the day Porca moves about the place, fluttering along the tops of the shutters, work surfaces, people's shoulders and heads and, in fine weather, all around the farm. His flying skills are a sight to see, particularly in the house where he has to make tight turns, sudden climbs and fast changes of direction to negotiate obstacles he finds in his path – unexpectedly closed doors, or cats and dogs with intentions inimical to his well-being.

He can stop and turn in the air with amazing precision, and he has developed a clever strategy for getting through the fly-curtain. He used to land, walk through the curtain, and take off again, but that was an opportunity for the cats to have a crack at him, so he laboriously perfected the technique of landing on the curtain, parting the strings of beads with his feet, poking his head and body through the parting, then dropping through the other side and, with a flurry of wing-beats, lifting off before he hits the mat.

Besides his devotion to Ana, Porca's other obsession is nesting. For a time we wondered if we had got his gender wrong, but in fact it is the males who do most of the building in the parrot world. For days on end, Porca would busy himself flying about the house and garden, gathering a baffling assortment of odds and ends: chopsticks, baler-twine, bits of paper, twigs, biros and toothbrushes. It's difficult to know how parrots get hold of these needments in the jungles of Brazil.

Once they had been gathered, he would arrange all of these materials in a manner that defied even the most vivid imagination to see any semblance of a nest. Some of the objects would be propped up against the legs of a chair; the string would be woven among legs and chopsticks; a plastic nailbrush would take pride of place in the centre; and to maintain a delicate architectural balance, wisps of dead grass would be laid artlessly here and there.

Porca would work on, earnestly and furiously, impervious to my sniggering over his efforts. It was cruel of me to ridicule him as his incompetence doubtless stemmed from being born in captivity, and from his having parents who either didn't know, or were unable to pass on, the information he needed. However, I feel sure that Porca, had he been suitably equipped, would laugh uproariously at anyone else's misfortunes and inadequacies.

Outside the house, Porca tends to perch in the acacia tree, where he pointedly ignores the pigeons – lowly creatures – or mucks about on his bird-table, a rustic sort of a thing that I lashed up for him in the hopes that I might one day be able to perform my ablutions in the bathroom in peace.

Sometimes, he takes great long swooping flights down over the farm and into the valley. Ana sees Porca as a sort of falcon. She stands on the edge of the terrace as he perches on her arm awaiting command. Then, with a deft flick of her wrist, she sends him hurtling and squawking down into the valley. 'Wheee-eee!' she cries. Porca moves like a rocket and when the sun catches his wings he flashes green like a passing emerald.

Domingo was navigating his way up the Cádiar river one morning, mounted on his donkey, when he was astonished to see a flutter of green wings and the arrival of the parrot, whom he hardly knew. Porca stood between the donkey's huge ears, like a pilot guiding a ship up a river, gazed at the scenery for a while, then rose with a squawk and flew away. Nowadays, he quite often flies off to perch on Domingo's shoulder down in the river fields and watches him working. Domingo feeds him *habas*, broad beans, which Porca adores and takes daintily from his fingers.

I tried this once and once only.

Near the end of Porca's first summer, however, he did something guaranteed to win even my sympathies. He got himself stepped on by a horse.

Even now, I'm not quite sure how it happened. I was helping Pepe the blacksmith shoe Lola when I sensed something just a touch greener than the grass, fooling around on the ground. I've never understood the attraction that hoof-shavings have for animals, but the dogs go crazy for the taste, and Porca must have been vying with them for a stake. Then Pepe banged the last clinch home and I let the horse's leg drop. A heart-rending screech rent the air. Porca was pinned beneath Lola, squawking, flapping and trying to tear himself from the monstrous hoof.

Lola of course was quite unaware that anything was going on at all down around her hindquarters, and stood firm and square. It took me a second of two to register what had happened. I leaned heavily on her and heaved the leg up. Porca shot out in a flurry of wings and, screeching like a banshee, flew up towards the house.

By the time I arrived panting in the kitchen, the room had become a tableau of grief. Poor damaged Porca was lying miserably on Ana's breast, his head on her neck, while she looked down at him, stricken with worry, and stroked his ruffled back feathers. Chloë, who had suffered almost as much from the parrot as me, was desolate; we all were. I thought Porca had a chance of surviving because of the energy he put into flying away from the accident, but there was no doubt that he was a much-reduced parakeet. All his aggression and his posturing machismo had gone, as he lay limp and sad, looking with woeful adoration up at his beloved Ana's face.

The atmosphere at home remained subdued through most of that week. It seemed that Porca's foot was so horribly mangled he might never be able to use it again. Now a parrot is a thing with three useful limbs: the wings are good for flying but not much else, while its beak and its feet are used for locomotion and feeding – one foot is used to hold the food, the other for balancing, and the beak for chopping it up. And then there's cleaning, where both the beak and the feet are used for preening. With only one foot left to stand on, Porca wouldn't be able to reach the feathers on the back of his head, and as parrots are very fastidious about grooming, he would go into a decline.

The feeding we solved by means of a wire with a little crocodile clip on one end and the other set in a block of plastic – a name plate, apparently, for dinner parties, which had mysteriously found its way into our cutlery drawer. But Ana worried that in his debilitated state Porca would be easy prey for the cats, who would be eager to get their own back after the humiliations he had heaped upon them. Ana reckoned the night-time was when they would make their move, as Porca couldn't fly at night and would stay put where he was as soon as the lights went out. She solved this problem by taking the parrot to bed.

He started out in a sort of a nest on the bedpost but before long had flopped down and worked his way between the sheets, tucking himself beneath the duvet with Ana. This of course presented a serious conflict of interests, as it was where I wanted to be too, and I felt I had prior claim. However, if I were foolish enough to edge over towards Ana's half of the bed, Porca would squawk and lay into me with his beak and peck me hard. It was about as bad as a thing can be for matrimonial harmony.

Defying all expectations, Porca's mangled leg started to mend and gain strength. First he began tentatively to tap it on his perch, and soon after he started to put weight upon it. Ana, as well as nourishing him with the warmth of her love – she would carry him about her waist in a sort of marsupial pouch – gave him healing balms recommended by her tomes on herbal medicine. Kate, a homeopathic doctor friend, helped us out with a course of specially customised little white pills. She seemed rather pleased to have an opportunity to add a parrot to her list of satisfied clients and suggested that we might also try to treat his aggression. You can do just about anything, she said, with homeopathy.

Sadly, Kate's nostrums were nothing against Porca's inherent swinishness. As soon as his foot improved he reverted to his old tricks, flying out of nowhere to savage me or Chloë for no reason at all. Most of his malevolent energy, however, was reserved for terrifying our guests. Porca has an unerring ability to spot the one person who is the most frightened of parrots and swoops towards them, beak poised to grab at an earlobe or clump of hair. For a lorophobe – and there are plenty of them around – this sort of treatment is beyond endurance.

The homeopathy did, however, seem to have one curious side-effect. It changed Porca's architectural interests from wood, as his main nesting material, to metal. He became suddenly a formidably armed creature, hurtling to and fro in the air with a pair of nail scissors dangling from his beak, or a steel trussing-needle with which he bombed the cats. Off went the car-keys, a flow of small change – the twenty-five peseta piece has a hole in the middle and makes a simply marvellous addition to any nest – and most of the kitchen cutlery.

These activities left the kitchen denuded of cutlery, and if anyone but Ana were foolish enough to stoop and borrow, say, a teaspoon, Porca would launch a ferocious attack. But the metalwork made the nests look slightly more interesting, albeit, to my untrained eye, unpromising places to nurture little parakeets.

As well as being violent, aggressive and bone-headed, Porca is also insistently demanding, like a child. He can't actually speak, which is probably a blessing, but he does a passing imitation of *Que pasa?* (What's happening?) and has a quiet *meep* noise which for a fleeting moment makes him seem quite sweet and appealing. There's also a special cooing sound that he uses in an attempt to entice Ana into one of his newly-created nests. *Chick-a-cheeoo, Chick-a-cheeo*, he croons while gazing imploringly into Ana's eyes. Now, Ana is not what you'd call a big woman but the chance of her fitting into Porca's nest beneath the kitchen shelf is almost as remote as her laying the longed-for egg.

Porca's demands reach fever pitch when Ana and I take a siesta and shut him out of the room. In order to catch our attention when we're just slipping away into sleep during the hottest hours of the day, he has hit upon the notion of perching on the utensil-rack above the cooker. The cooker is made of tin and it makes a pleasing crash when hit by, say, a heavy steel ladle, or the fish-slice or the big serving spoon. When Porca has finished nudging all the utensils off the rack – there are ten or so to get through – he flies to the bathroom door and sits on the handle squawking fit to bust. He can carry on squawking for ten whole minutes without stopping, and it's a sound that could easily wake, and considerably annoy, the dead.

A lie-in of a morning is not much easier to achieve, for Porca has learned how to open the bathroom door. As mentioned, he spends the night roosting on the shower tap in the bathroom, and as soon as it is light enough for him to fly, he opens the door – not quite as much of an achievement as it sounds, because I accidentally fitted the door backwards, so you only have to push it to open it, but have to operate the handle to close it. Anyway, Porca gets down on the floor and with all his tiny might, heaves and pushes until it opens. He then flies over to our bed, pecks me on whatever part of my body he finds protruding from the bedclothes, and having succeeded in driving me away, proceeds to get suggestive with Ana on the pillow. Grumbling and grunting, I shamble to the kitchen to put the kettle on. When I take Ana her morning cup of tea I get attacked again by the parrot. And thus starts another day.

Though Porca's talent lies in destruction, there are just a few positive aspects to having him around. For one, he's a constant source of fascination, even in his choice of loco-motion – flying, hitching lifts on people and animals, riding head down in Ana's pocket, or walking brazenly along the floor, ignoring the predatory stares of the dogs and cats – it all adds spice to our lives here. For another, Porca seems in a perverse way to be licking us all into shape. I've noticed that I've become distinctly less confrontational with Porca around. It has been ages now since it occured to me to place the blue toothmug on the washing machine cover. Chloë, too, seems to have become more philosophical about life's random injustices, particularly those taking the form of parrot attacks, while Ana seems to cope reasonably well with being treated as the acme of perfection.

There's no doubt about it. Much as Porca makes me suffer, I'd find it hard not to have a parrot in the family now.

ETHICS AND
ANTI-CLERICALISM

'HOMBRE! YOU'VE GOT TO BE JOKING! I can't get past there. This is a car, not a mule. I'll wait.' There was a lorry slewed across the track, its ramp down on the bank. Four men were trying to persuade a bullock to get in, but understandably it didn't want to go. Standing tethered nearby was the mother of the bullock, a gentle liquid-eyed creature with horns and a soft wet muzzle. She watched the proceedings with sad incomprehension.

The lorry belonged to Antonio, Manolo's cousin. The cattle belonged to Juan Díaz, who farms up on Carrasco.

'Are you getting a good price for him, Juan?' I asked.

'No, Cristóbal. Price not good. Farmers very, very poor. Butcher very rich man.'

'That always seems to be the way. He's a beautiful bull.'

'Beautiful bull. Big big balls.' And he patted the pendulous bag. 'Very delicious eat. He boy. Mummy there.' He indicated the cow. 'She come make him happy.'

Juan Díaz is a man who knows his farming. His farm is a delight to visit, always green and trim and well cultivated, with healthy trees and fine crops. It is just down the valley from Bernardo, who speaks Alpujarran Spanish as fluently as anyone I've met, but is treated by Juan, like the rest of us foreigners, as if he were on his first day at language school.

Bernardo told me how one day he was standing around, talking to Domingo, when Juan Díaz appeared, striding round the bend on his way back from town.

'Morning Juan. Not a bad day,' offered Bernardo.

'No rain. Very bad, very bad. Sun pretty but not good. Trees and plants dry. Farmers poor.'

'I heard the forecast this morning. They say there's a possibility of rain towards the end of the week.'

'Maybe rain. Maybe not rain. We not know...'

Domingo, who had been staring in bafflement at Juan during this exchange, interrupted. 'Why in the name of the Host are you talking in that strange way, Juan? I've never heard anything like it! Bernardo here is not a half-wit.'

'No. Not half-wit. Foreigner, not Spanish. Not understand.'

'But Bernardo speaks Spanish as well as you or I do.'

Juan was in a difficult predicament here; he didn't know whether to speak normally for Domingo, or to maintain the pidgin Spanish for the benefit of poor benighted Bernardo, who might speak good Spanish, but was unalterably a foreigner.

Anyway, Domingo's criticism made not the slightest difference. Juan never speaks to a foreigner except in his extraordinary baby talk. I have quite long conversations with him sometimes, when I give him a lift into town for example. His strangely reduced speech drives me to seek out the most colloquial expressions that I can find.

'Morning Juan, hop in, save you a bit of a walk.'

'Very kind, Cristóbal. Orgiva far. Juan old. Legs bad.'

'And what takes you to town on this lovely morning, Juan?'

'You do, Cristóbal, in your car. Very big, very fast.'

'No, I mean why are you going?'

'See doctor. Juan ill.'

'What's the matter with you?'

'Hands hurt. Not work well.' He showed me his huge cracked hands. 'Too much work, cold water. Also legs bad.'

And on we go. If I live near Juan for the rest of my life, he will never address me in any other manner. But it is meant kindly: a language contrived to be as considerate as possible to a linguistic simpleton. Juan manages to speak almost entirely without recourse to verbs, and on the odd occasion when there is no other way out, he uses only the simple form. The nouns are kept basic, and the article, definite or indefinite, is omitted.

This form of speech might be undemanding, but it's also severely limiting. You can't get very deep into abstract subjects without using verbs.

One autumn night a badger came and ravaged our vegetable patch. I wandered over the river and told Bernardo my woes. 'The man you should talk to about badgers,' he said at once, 'is Juan Diáz. He knows all there is to know about them.' So I set off to talk to Juan about the badger problem. Chloë, who goes to school with a Diáz granddaughter, came along for the ride.

We found Juan grubbing up the little walnut trees that had sown themselves all over his terraces. He straightened up, brushed some of the dirt from his hand and gave Chloë a fond pat. '*Hola, guapisima!*' he greeted her – 'Hello, Most Beautiful.'

Then he turned to me with a concentrated smile on his face. 'Big tree. Little babies. One day big trees, too,' he said, indicating the saplings. 'You plant at El Valero. Babies now, one day walnut forest.' As an aside to Chloë he asked, 'Do you think your mother would like some? She has a way with trees.'

Like many of our neighbours, Juan makes a distinction between Chloë, born and bred in the Alpujarras, and rank outsiders like ourselves. Chloë's accent helps, of course – she speaks Spanish with the slightly lisping style, thin on consonants, that's favoured in these parts, and she peppers it with playground idioms. Ana and I could never hope to catch up.

'That's very kind,' I broke in, nonetheless. 'Ana loves walnut trees. But Juan, we have come to see you on this fine afternoon because we have a problem with a badger – well, I think it's a badger at any rate. It's eating our vegetables. Bernardo says you know all about badgers. So do you have any idea what we can do to keep this one off the vegetable patch?'

'Badger very bad. Motorcycle clutch cable...' Juan drew a circle in the air and mimed pulling it tight.

'Pardon?'

'Moto clutch cable. Very good thing. With moto clutch you kill him good and dead.'

'There must be something more to it than that? You've omitted to explain something, perhaps?' I asked, a little pompously.

'It's to make a trap with, Daddy,' Chloë hissed. 'The badger runs into it and gets caught, maybe even strangled.' She fixed me with her sternest expression as she said this. Chloë and Ana share some very firm opinions on the morality of traps, though in deference to Juan, she was trying to keep these to herself.

'Chloë right,' Juan added, beaming obliviously. Then, as if all his fears had been confirmed about having to communicate with the intellectual dregs of Europe, he continued miming and mouthing his explanation. 'Find where badger come. Same place always. Clutch cable in path, badger come, neck through loop – caught! Bang! Dead! Simple, no?'

'Yes,' I answered. 'But why do you need a clutch cable?'

Juan gave me that look people use when they decide to start painstakingly from the beginning again.

'Daddy wants to know why you chose a clutch cable rather than anything else?' Chloë lisped, rushing to the rescue.

'Because there's a heap of them going begging in the road outside Daniel's moto repair shop and they'll do as well as anything else,' Juan confided to her.

So that was how you dealt with the badger problem, clearly and succinctly explained. Yet there was one niggling matter still left unresolved. 'Chloë?' I asked, as we bumped our way back across the ford in the river. 'Do you know the Spanish for snare?'

Chloë made a face. 'No I don't, and I don't think I want to either. They're horrid things, Daddy, and really hurt the animals. We shouldn't use anything like that at El Valero,' she announced and then resumed sucking thoughtfully the boiled sweet that Juan had spirited out of the pocket of his overalls.

Though I like to think that my Spanish vocabulary has, by now, expanded to fit most of the needs of Alpujarran living, I have discovered that it is – well – full of snares.

Animals, particularly, are a sea of uncertainty. *Comadreja, garduña, jineta, gato clavo, hurón,* are all names of creatures that exist in an area of uncertain identities, often distinguished only by the size of hole they can squeeze through to get at your poultry. I'm sure similar confusions exist with the English equivalent – stoats, weasels, martens, jennets, ferrets, and so on.

Then, if you move one size or so down the ladder of threatening animals you arrive in the even more interesting linguistic territory of the *bichos*. Now, *bicho* is one of my favourite Spanish words. It should refer to creatures round about the insect size bracket – as in 'there are *bichos* in this bed and they are eating me alive' – but it can be expanded to encompass smallish non-insects, like rodents, and under exceptional circumstances its borders might even stretch to a cat or even a dog. With the licence that being a foreigner and having a wretchedly imperfect grasp of the language permits me, I have even managed a cow and a horse, and by adding the suffix *–aco* have made the thing sound formidable, menacing even. '*Vaya bicharaco!*' I might exclaim – 'Blimey, what a creature!'

Yet these are all minor linguistic inconveniences, compared to the minefield of the written letter or note.

If you live your whole life in the country you were born in, you are unlikely to be greatly taxed by the problem of writing notes to school bus drivers. Of course you may have to do it, but you will probably be able to dash it off without a moment's thought:

> *To Whom it May Concern:*
>
> *My daughter, Chloë, will not be returning with the school bus this afternoon as she will be engaged in after-school activities in town. Thank you for your co-operation.*
>
> *Yours sincerely, Christopher Stewart (father).*

I imagine they go something like that, dashed off in haste, though I'm not altogether sure as I've never had to do one in English. Here in Andalucia, it's very different.

'Chris, can you write a note for the school bus driver?' Ana asked one day. It was not an unfamiliar request.

'Why, dear?' I answered, stalling as usual.

'Because Chloë is staying after school tomorrow with Alba-Teresa and Laura-María.'

'Can't we just tell the driver?'

'No, we really have to do it properly. You must remember what happened before?'

Ana was referring to an occasion on which we were blamed for keeping six children incarcerated on a bus on a sweltering afternoon, all because we had failed to pass on a note saying that Chloë was staying behind for a dance class.

The fact that Ana had already alerted the bus driver to this on two separate occasions was of no account. Poor Chloë had to suffer a week of frosty looks and comments from the assembled parents before the spotlight fell onto some other poor noteless sap. So these days we always write to the school bus driver and to Mari-Carmen who is the loader and checker at the school end.

'Well, why can't you write the note then?' I countered.

'Because I'm busy and, besides, I thought you were supposed to be the writer in the family.'

Ana's dig seemed a little below the belt but I resigned myself to the task and set to finding a suitable piece of paper to write the note on. The paper shouldn't be too big, as the sort of note I planned to write wouldn't occupy very much space, and a big piece of paper would draw attention to this. It shouldn't be too small either, as this would give an impression of impecuniousness or, worse, meanness – neither of which are the sort of impression you want to make on school bus drivers. Having unsuccessfully combed the house and all its outbuildings for the right-sized piece of paper, I hit on the notion of cutting one to the exact dimensions required – creating a sort of bespoke bus driver's note page. The cutting, of course, had to be just so. I tried with our ancient pair of scissors, some knives, a ruler, folding and tearing.

Eventually I achieved the perfect piece of paper, found my pen, and sat down to compose. I thought for a bit. *Muy Pino mio*, I wrote – 'Very Pine Mine.' This was a standard beginning but I didn't like it much; something didn't quite click, and besides I wasn't sure who was driving the bus that week. There were three potential drivers: Pino, Moya, or Jordi. It was too late to ask Chloë, who was fast asleep.

I crossed out *Muy Pino mio* – but no, that was no good, I couldn't have crossings out. I crumpled the paper and took up another sheet. This time I'd do it first in rough. A part of the problem is that Spanish letter writing has a tendency to be rather formal, and the writing of formal business Spanish seems to be mired in lunacy. I caught a whiff of business Spanish once in a book I was learning from, and just that brief exposure seems to have contaminated my style.

Estimado señor – 'Esteemed Sir' – I began again. It had a nice ring to it but was perhaps a bit heavy. It would have to go. I crossed it out and with a flourish wrote *Querido amigo*, 'Beloved Friend.' I considered this uncertainly for a while, doubting its literary merit. And that was another problem; people in town knew that I had had some success abroad as a writer, so the contents of this note might not just be between me and the adressee. There was the awful possibility that the note would be passed around all the bus drivers to be mulled over, criticised, admired or reviled. In my worst, most paranoid, imaginings I could see my note pinned to the public notice board in the Ayuntamiento, the Town Hall, as an example. I had to get this right.

I thought hard about the note for some time with no success. Then I drank my share of a bottle of wine to see if I could find any inspiration there, but it only induced a desire to go to bed. Probably the inspiration would come during the night and I could just dash it off in the morning. Of course I spent the night rolling about in anguish, tormented by various combinations of address. 'Esteemed Friend, Beloved Sir, Most Excellent Bus Driver... Very Bus Driver Mine...'

Next morning I rose early to prepare Ana's morning cup of tea, get Chloë's breakfast, and do some more work on the note. *Hola Jordi*, I started. Chloë had told me that Jordi was on this week, and Jordi, being younger and more modern than Pino or Moya, would more than likely be happy with a less formal approach. *Hi Jordi, With this letter I inform you that my daughter Chloë will not be returning with the school bus this evening, but will be staying on in town.*

I wasn't wild about the construction but it would have to do given the approaching deadline. 'Will not be returning': that ought really to be in the subjunctive as it referred to an act contemplated in an uncertain future and was also referred to at one remove. That seemed like a good case for a subjunctive. But it would be such a bunfight dredging up the appropriate subjunctive that I decided to let it slide. Jordi wouldn't mind.

But how to finish the note? It wasn't a business letter, and I knew Jordi pretty well, so it wouldn't be necessary to roll out all the ornate religious stuff about 'God Guarding the Recipient Through Many Years' – a formal but surprisingly common sign-off in Spanish letters. This left the following options: *atentamente* (sincerely), *un saludo* (a salute), *un abrazo* (a hug), *un beso* or *besos* (a kiss or kisses). This last I dismissed out of hand. I liked Jordi but not quite that much.

Un saludo, Cristóbal.

With a sigh of relief I hunted about for an envelope, then headed off to take Chloë to the school bus. I was pleased to discover that it was indeed being driven by Jordi.

'Morning, Jordi, here's a note for you,' I announced.

'Oh yeah, what's it about?'

'It's just to tell you that Chloë isn't coming on the school bus this afternoon.'

'OK. I'll remember that.'

'Yes, but take the note.'

'But you've just told me. I don't need the note.'

'Go on, take the note.'

'No. What do I need a note for?'

'It's the proper way to do it... I have to give you a note.'

'It's really not necessary, Cristóbal...'

'Look, Jordi, I've been up half the bleeding night writing this note, I'm certainly not going to take it home with me.'

'*Tranquilo, Cristóbal, tranquilo.* There, I've got your note.' And he took the envelope and stuffed it in the sun visor.

Satisfied with a job well done, I stood and watched as the bus disappeared round the cliff in a cloud of dust and a rattle and clank of the loose fittings. Had I known what further authorial chores awaited, I'd have been a lot less complacent.

One of the reasons that Ana had no time for notewriting was that she was preparing to meet her mother for the weekend in Malaga, leaving me to look after Chloë, the farm and animals. I fed the livestock and, before settling down for a long day's grind staring at the computer, set about making some pancake mix for Chloë. If you do pancakes you can always get children on your side, which I find sets the whole business of childcare off on the right footing.

At six I headed across the valley to fetch Chloë from a schoolfriend's house. 'Guess what we're having for supper tonight,' I said as we walked together down to the river.

'Pancakes, I expect,' she said, rather absently, then revived a little, adding, 'Ooh lovely, my favourite.'

There was clearly something preying on her mind.

'Daddy?' she asked, after a pause.

'Yes?'

'Daddy, you promise not to be angry if I ask you something?'

'I'll try to promise, though it does depend on what it is you want to ask me.'

'Well... I want to stop going to *religión* classes. I just don't like them anymore. Can I stop, Daddy? Can I?'

'There's no reason I should be angry about a thing like that, is there? I'll tell you what, we'll have a talk about it when your mother gets home.' Normally I can stave off thorny issues with this simple delaying device, but Chloë wasn't going to be sidetracked this time.

'But it's *religión* on Friday and I don't want to go. Can you go and talk to the teacher about it? Please, Daddy, please.'

We had reached the bridge by this time so conversation was momentarily suspended while we picked our way along the timber beams above a torrent of white water.

The *religión* question was by no means new. When Chloë had first joined the school we had thought long and hard over whether to keep her in the Religious Education class or plump for *ética* on the grounds of my confirmed agnosticism. We had decided in the end that an insider's knowledge of the Bible and the tenets of Christianity would be more of a help than a hindrance in getting to grips with European literature and culture. It also seemed a good way to get a grounding in the numerous festivals and saint's days that pepper the Alpujarran calendar.

A glance through the *religión* school books satisfied us that the opposition were getting a fair crack of the whip. There were brief accounts of other faiths accompanied by caricatures of people of a dusky hue with bulging eyes wearing loin cloths and sitting about in the lotus position. Mohammed and the Muslims got pretty short shrift if I remember rightly – too close for comfort in Andalucia – but the more oriental religions were assumed to be far enough away not to pose a threat. These books were obviously not produced with the Alpujarras in mind, however. All the oriental religions are well represented here and within ten kilometres of Orgiva there are more cults and sects and sub-sects than you can wave a joss stick at.

I questioned my daughter a little more. 'Why are you so against *religión*, Chloë?'

'*Religión* is boring and I just don't really like it and *ética* is much more interesting.'

'Ah, but how do you know it's more interesting?'

'Hannah told me.'

'Of course, she must know quite a bit about it by now.' Hannah is Chloë's best friend. She's German and her parents are rather progressive, so Hannah got opted out of the religious classes from the very start.

'And Zohra, too,' Chloë added. Zohra is another close friend of Chloë's, and as you might deduce from the name, is a Muslim.

'And Alba Recio.' Alba Recio's parents are Spanish progressive. The picture was becoming clearer now. Chloë liked the idea of being part of the exclusive little coterie, sitting apart and studying ethics, while the lumpen masses droned through catechisms and learned how to tell their rosary beads. I was impressed, and as we sat and ate our pancakes together, I mused out loud about what an interesting subject ethics was.

Chloë agreed wholeheartedly and before she went to bed we read two chapters from *Heidi*, a favourite of Chloë's at that time. I'd hoped to fit in a discussion about the different ethical universes of Grandfather and Fräulein Rottenmeier, but we got engrossed in the astonishingly curative effects of toasted cheese and mountain air on Clara's disability. I did note, however, that Chloë showed no absolute objection to Grandfather returning to the village church and hob-nobbing with the vicar.

The next night, when Ana arrived home, I told her about our discussion. 'Are you sure she doesn't just want to have an hour off to fool around with her friends', she said.

Ana can be shockingly suspicious at times. But she did agree that it would be hypocritical of us to force Chloë to continue with religion if she'd specifically opted for ethics and that we should, perhaps, swing behind our daughter on this one. Personally, I was delighted with Chloë's anti-clerical stance and thought it boded well for a free-thinking future. So the next afternoon I went along to see her teacher, Don Manuel.

Chloë horsed around in the playground while I was sent up the stairs to do the deal. Don Manuel was very under-standing, but, he said, there was a problem: it was late in the spring term and, normally, if you wanted to drop a subject you should do it at the beginning of the school year. It was the sort of irregularity that might have everyone jumping on the same wagon, because, he confided in me, there were quite a few who wanted to change classes. *Ética*, it seemed, was becoming increasingly popular among the pupils.

'Oh, Don Manuel,' I said, '*porfi?*' – I had found myself using the children's abbreviation of *por favor*.

'Look, I'll tell you what we'll do. We'll go and see *El Director*, Don Antonio, and see if he suggests anything. How about that?'

'Fine', I said, 'that's fine with me,' and I was taken along to the headmaster's study. I hadn't been in one of these for years, and was amazed to find myself gnawing away at the corner of my thumbnail. But Don Antonio had a friendly intelligent manner that soon put me at my ease. We shook hands warmly.

'How can I help you?' he asked

I looked at Don Manuel and Don Manuel looked at me. Then he stated my case.

'Yes, that's it exactly,' I said.

'Alright then,' said Don Antonio slowly. 'But tell me just why you want your daughter to do *ética* rather than *religión?*'

I coughed, buying time. 'Well, it's like this...' and I offered Don Antonio a halting argument about humanist ideals and a wish to encourage Chloë to think beyond the constraints of religion.

'That seems reasonable to me,' he said. 'But you do see Manuel's problem, don't you? If we extend this privilege to your daughter, then the whole lot will want out of *religión* and into *ética. Ética* is a very popular subject, you know.'

'So I've been told,' I answered.

'But I'll tell you what,' said *El Director*. 'You write me a letter stating succinctly your reasons for removing Chloë from the religion class, and I will make an exception for you.'

'You shall have it by Monday morning,' I said.

'What did he say, Daddy, what did he say?' I wonder why children have to repeat everything.

'Well, I went to see the *Director* and he said that if I can write him a good letter, then he'll let you move to *ética*.'

'Oh Daddy, thank you, thank you.'

'But you'll have to go to *religión* on Friday, I'm not going to finish the letter that soon.'

'I don't mind, Daddy, I don't mind at all.'

I had the rest of the week and the weekend to get the letter done. And I needed every minute. This was the big league, a philosophical essay to the Head Teacher. I was going to need time to build up a pace, go down some blind alleys and recover myself or explore my central thesis from a range of angles.

I sharpened my pencil, poured myself a drink, and set about killing a few flies. Then I opened my book, scraped some candlewax off the table, and picked up the newspaper.

I awoke with a start as a voice impinged upon my reverie.

'Are you writing that letter to the *Director*, Daddy?'

'Er, yes, as a matter of fact I am.'

'Can I see what you've written?'

'It's not much yet – it just says *Estimado don Antonio*.'

'In Spanish, you write *Don* with a capital letter.'

'Oh, you do, do you?'

'You haven't got very far with it yet, have you?' Chloë added, picking up her felt pens and moving to the far end of the room.

Soon, though, the muse started to take control, and I banged off three or four tolerable paragraphs. As I sat back and admired them, Ana came in.

'How's the essay going?' she asked, and then, seeing that I was on to my second page, added, 'Finished with the Counter-Reformation, yet?' There was a definite smirk playing around the corners of her mouth. Chloë, however, had jumped up with an anxious look on her face.

'It's not going at all badly, in spite of interruptions.' I waved the page airily in Ana's direction – a foolish move as I hadn't meant her to read it just yet.

Ana's look changed to one of furrowed concentration. 'Chris, you can't say that...' she announced, taking hold of the sheet.

'What can't he say?' asked Chloë, moving across to the table.

'Look, who's writing this letter, for heaven's sake?!'

'It's too obscure, Chris. I don't think anyone will understand what on earth you're on about,' said Ana, in all seriousness now.

'Oh Daddy, please do it properly – please Daddy.'

'What exactly do you mean, for instance,' continued Ana, 'by *the distortion of children's natural striving toward the Numinous*? Where on earth has all this come from?'

She had a point. 'Maybe you're right...'

'But do you know what it means?'

'Er... I read it in a book, it's about being awed by the presence of the divine.' In truth it didn't sound much more convincing in the author's own voice.

'Daddy!' came an exasperated splutter from Chloë. 'What's THAT got to do with anything – and it's *la razon*, not *el razon* – don't you know *anything*?'

Then, with a concentrated look on her face, Chloë began to dictate, stressing each word with a wave of her felt pen. 'Why don't you just say that you want me to grow up to be a good citizen in a thingy... uh... secular society. And you think *ética* can teach me that best.' She finished with a dramatic rap of her pen on the table and then dragged her seat towards me to supervise the secretarial work.

I was dumbfounded. Even Ana had an eyebrow raised. If this change of lessons could bring out such rhetoric from my daughter, then it was surely worthwhile.

'Chloë,' I gasped. 'That's brilliant. That's an amazingly good argument – simple, to-the-point...'

'Well,' Chloë shrugged. 'It worked for Hannah and Alba Recio. I don't see why I shouldn't say it too?'

On Monday morning I stuffed the letter into the most respectable-looking envelope I could find and sent it to school with Chloë. 'If you lose this letter, then you're stuck with *religión* for life,' I admonished her.

Next day Chloë returned from school in a state of euphoria. 'Don Manuel says I don't have to go to *religión* any more,' she said. 'Thank you, Daddy, thank you.'

I was really rather pleased.

Later that week I saw Hannah's mother, Tina, in town. Tina is an attractive, energetic woman who runs a doctor's surgery and a farm with her husband. However, she's never too busy to stop and talk and it's always a pleasure.

'Chloë's thrilled to be joining the *ética* class with Hannah,' I announced. I thought of adding a brief account of my letter-writing efforts but it seemed gratuitous.

'Uh-huh,' said Tina, as if waiting for the main subject.

This piqued me slightly. 'I'm a bit worried,' I persevered, 'that she might find herself quite far behind the rest of the class. She hasn't been given any course books yet, you see.'

'Course books?' Tina looked at me incredulously. 'But she's doing *ética*.'

'I know, but they must have some sort of reference book?'

'Chris,' she said, looking at me with the same incredulous look. 'You do know what *ética* is? Don't you?'

'Well, I think so, I've put together a pretty good argument as to why Chloë should do it...' But I never did get to repeat Chloë's rhetoric because Tina's next words took the wind from my sails.

'It's colouring-in, Chris.'

'Urp', I gulped. 'So no debates on morality, then?'

'No, Chris, just... crayons.'

BACK TO SCHOOL

ONE OF THE THINGS that had prompted Ana and me to settle in Andalucia was our shared love of flamenco. Before arriving here we both had visions of going off to Granada for all-night sessions at flamenco clubs, while I nurtured the idea of reviving the guitar-lessons of my youth at the feet of some local maestro. In the event, we've seen an awful lot more shepherds than guitarists during our time here. Either it's been too hard to find someone to look after the animals, or we hadn't wanted to haul Chloë into dark, smoky bars, or the money just wouldn't stretch. In fact, the sad truth is that most of our exposure to the top-notch Andalucian players has been through tapes kindly sent by friends in Madrid.

As luck would have it, though, Chloë has developed her own love of flamenco dance – or, to be more exact, a love of *Sevillanas*, the castanet-clacking fare of every Andalucian fiesta. From an early age she would stand spellbound at the front of a stage, studying every movement of the dancers. Later, when we bought her first flamenco dress, it thrilled me to see her swirling, clapping or stomping along with them. I had hoped that her enthusiasm might have prompted her to pick up the guitar but, sadly, she has resisted all my attempts to interest her in the instrument. Sadder still, and painfully resonant of my Seville days, she appears to prefer the accompaniment of a cassette tape to her dad.

The local maestros all failed to materialise, too. None of the country folk who would occasionally stay for a drink and a *tapa* on our terrace showed the slightest inclination to pull down one of the guitars which hung on our walls. Even Domingo, who seems able to turn his hand to anything, proved oblivious to this part of his heritage. '*Me da igual,*' he said, using that bleak Andalucian phrase – 'it's all the same to me' – when I got my guitar down and asked if he enjoyed music.

So, when Ben rang to say he'd like to come and stay, and would be bringing his guitar, I skipped like a lamb. 'That's great, Ben,' I burbled. 'Yes, by all means, come just whenever you like, and stay for good.'

Since I had never met Ben before, the offer, as Ana pointed out, was perhaps a bit rash. But I had heard about him. He was the nephew of a very close friend in London and had come to Spain to do just what I should have been doing: learn proper flamenco technique at a guitar school in Granada.

Ben arrived the morning after his phone call and before the sun had set on his dusty yellow 2CV he had become that rare thing, the indispensable guest. He was utterly disarming – tall, blond, with a cultured air and aquiline nose – like some character washed up by the sea from the classical world. For three weeks he dazzled us all: Ana with his conversation and charm; Chloë by being fun and introducing her to a whole new set of tricks and clapping games; and me with his guitar playing, which filled me with inspiration. During his month at flamenco school Ben had picked up an impressive repertoire which he played with an easy fluidity, and the lovely sound of his guitar washed over us all like a stream across a bed of pebbles.

El Valero is made for guitar music: 'If I were really rich,' I had often thought to myself, 'I would employ a minstrel.' Ben was the next best thing, but a few months earlier I had in fact almost acquired a minstrel. His name was Ángel – and it suits him, for I have met few souls quite so ethereal.

I ran into Ángel one winter evening, near the house of a Muslim family at the top end of the valley. 'You wouldn't by any chance have a job for me, would you?' he asked.

'Well, I can give you all the work you want,' I assured this gentle-looking spectre. 'But I'm afraid there's no money to pay you. Why, what do you do anyway?'

'Well man, I play guitar and I can sing, and I guess I'm something of an artist – and I'm really good at *yeso*, plastering.'

I was a little taken aback. Did Ángel really think that I would pay him to play guitar and sing to me – or even pay him to paint me pictures? *Yeso* was good – I could always use some plasterwork – but as I had said, I had no money for pay.

'I suppose the guitar playing would be quite a bit cheaper than the *yeso* work?' I enquired, idly.

'Oh yeah, man. I mean I really wouldn't charge a whole lot of money to play guitar for you.'

I sat in silence for a minute, taking this on board.

'When do I start?' asked Ángel brightly.

'I'm sorry, Ángel. I'd love to be the sort of guy who can employ a guitarist or an artist or a minstrel, but I'm afraid it's not going to happen in this life.'

I went on my way, leaving Ángel a little crestfallen.

Not long after Ben's all-too-brief stay, I signed up at the guitar school in Granada. This wasn't just Mr Toad-like suggestibility, but an emergency measure for the harmony of our home. Ana and Chloë, having sampled the higher plane of Ben's playing, were having a bit of difficulty adjusting back down to the earthier terrain of my own. Ana particularly was reaching the end of her tolerance of my constant practice sessions and would resort to acts of virtual warfare, ranging from the gratuitous use of a coffee grinder to incitement of the animals.

Then, one day, she cracked completely. I had been explaining how lucky she was to have a guitarist like me about the place to fill the house with sweet music – a little provocative, I own – when she turned on me.

'Chris, I really don't think you can call that music!' she said. 'It's absolutely intolerable and there's not a woman on the planet who'd put up with it. Bobble'obble'obble'obble all day long...' And she gave me a passable and even funny, imitation of a guitar doing a bad tremolo.

It took the wind out of my sails and I laughed. 'It's not funny,' she growled, keeping the tone censorious. 'What I suggest is that from now on you go and practise in the study or, better still, the sheep shed, and then, when you're good and ready you could give us a recital – once a week, at the most – and Chloë and I will listen, and maybe even clap.'

I turned to Chloë. I know it's wrong to put your daughter in the middle of a serious domestic rift, but this did also concern her. Her musical education was, after all, at risk. 'What do you think, Chloë?' I asked – she was sitting at the table concentrating rather too closely on her schoolwork – 'Do you think that's fair?'

Chloë looked distressed. She hated being placed in such a delicate diplomatic position. 'No, Daddy,' she mumbled. 'It's not.' Then with her hand disguising the giggle that was about to erupt, she added: 'Those poor, poor sheep.'

And so it was that one midwinter afternoon I strode out with my guitar and headed for Granada. I arrived in Orgiva just too late for the bus, so I walked out of town and stuck my thumb out. It was years since I'd last hitch-hiked but within three minutes I was speeding along, chatting away to a young *Granadina* on her way home to the city from a holiday in the Alpujarra.

The light was fading as I slogged my way up the Cuesta del Chápiz, where the school stood at the top of a steep cobbled hill. The climb warmed me a little; as the sun dropped behind the rooftops a wicked chill had crept through the streets of the city. Behind the great wooden door of the *Escuela Carmen de las Cuevas* was a pretty patio with pots of aspidistras and a little stone fountain. In the patio there milled about a motley gaggle of girls and boys, weaving uncertainly among each other's guitar-cases, wondering which language to speak.

At forty-eight I wasn't quite the old man of the class – that was Jean-Paul who was well into his fifties – but the rest were much younger: weekend musicians, students, drifters, a clown from Munich. They were a nice rag-bag of bohemians. However, I felt the discrepancy in age acutely. Images of Herb from my youthful years in Seville came flooding back and with them the slightly paranoid idea that my fellow students saw me as an anachronism, someone who had wandered onto the wrong stage set. Whenever anyone addressed a question or comment to me I couldn't help but feel that there was another question lurking beneath its surface – 'Hell, man, why bother?'

I even thought I detected an odd sort of look from Nacho, who ran the place, when I went into the office to register. Leaning my guitar against the wall I smiled indulgently when he asked which course I intended to take. 'Well, I'm certainly not a beginner,' I assured him. 'I mean I've been playing for almost thirty years.'

'So what are you, then..?' asked Nacho.

A certain modesty, almost certainly misplaced, made me hesitate to put my name down for advanced class. 'I suppose I'd better go with the intermediates,' I said self-deprecatingly.

'Right, then,' said Nacho. 'Ten o'clock tomorrow, you'll be upstairs with Emilio.'

I went off, a little hesitantly, to the flat I had been assigned and, sitting on a chair in the icy kitchen, started practising for my first encounter with Emilio. In the other room I could hear the German clown, Horst, who had signed himself up for the beginners' class. Horst was getting a nice rounded tone from his guitar, and his tremolo was deliciously smooth.

I started into some thumb exercises that I hadn't done for years, and soon realised just what a slob my thumb had become. Next I did some gruelling *rasgueado* work, shooting each of my four fingers down hard across all the strings, making sure the little finger and the ring finger came down as strongly as their big brothers.

It was cold and getting colder. After an hour I could feel a nasty pain setting into the tiny muscles at the top of my ring finger. A nagging pain.

'Horst,' I called out. 'Let's get out of here, go find something to eat...' Horst, whose playing had been getting more sluggish and frozen by the minute, emerged stiffly from his room. We exchanged polite pleasantries about each other's playing, and headed out into the icy night to scour the Albaicin quarter in search of sustenance.

Horst was what the Spanish call *pesado* – a little 'heavy' or earnest – not unlike the clowns I'd known in the circus. Still, once we had found a restaurant, and a bottle of red wine was on the table, we both eased up, and soon I was hooting with laughter at his Teutonic line in scatological jokes.

That night, however, I was troubled by strange dreams in which Emilio and the intermediate students featured. We had run into a group of the intermediates on the way back from dinner. They were Americans, apart from a cheerful chap from somewhere in the bogs of the Low Countries, with the appealing name of Ale-Jan van Donk. Among the Americans were a couple of Californians called Brent and

Kirk, and a very tall man called Elin, who looked a bit like a warlock with his cloak-like overcoat and mane of shiny black hair. He looked even stranger in my dream, with long white fingers topped with plastic nails, and a hooked-back thumb – actually a not unusual deformity of flamenco guitarists. Crazy with energy, the dream Elin rapped out his *rasgueados* with those powerful plastic nails, with a sound like machine-gun fire.

My own dream playing was strangely doleful. I fear the technical term for it might have been geriatric.

It was with a certain trepidation that I pushed open the door of the classroom. The Californians were already playing and looked self-consciously cool as I entered and asked if this was Emilio's class. 'Yeah,' they said in unison and got their heads back down to their playing, crisp and neat, with perfect *compás* – rhythm and accents in all the right places.

Ale-Jan came in a few minutes later, grinned at me, looked a little disconcertedly at the Californians, and raised an eyebrow. And then at last the great man, Emilio, pitched into the room. A wiry gypsy with horn-rimmed glasses, long thinning hair, darting eyes and what looked like a cruel smile, he looked us over briefly, then clapped his hands to silence the guitars. 'Right! *Alegrías*. You all know it. Let's go!'

And they were off, or at least Brent and Kirk were off, ripping into a fast staccato piece. Ale-Jan and I awkwardly fingered our instruments. I didn't know *Alegrías* at all, and if I did I certainly wouldn't be able to play it like that.

Discreetly I slipped my guitar back in its case and sneaked cravenly out of the door before the piece had finished. Down the stairs I crept and into the cave where Nacho was putting the beginners through an *alzapúa* exercise – playing the string with both the downstroke and the upstroke of the thumb. He looked up at me and my thirty years of guitar playing with an amused but friendly grin and paused the class. 'Welcome, Maestro!' he greeted me.

I wanted to disappear into a corner but that was impossible. The cave where the beginners did their stuff was used for dance classes and the walls were lined with mirrors. This made my humiliating entrance all the more humiliating: not only could I see all those humble beginners looking up at me, but I could see myself seeing them seeing me, as if in a simultaneous re-run.

I took my place, though, and a few minutes later drew some comfort as Ale-Jan slunk in. I wasn't the only pretender.

The days of practice unfolded as we novices strived to follow Nacho's instructions, and to pick out the sound of his own playing amid our own. This wasn't easy since we all seemed to be playing just slightly out of sync, and as Nacho explained a finer point, there always seemed to be some silly bugger loudly practising the bit we had just learned.

Still, when we played through a piece we were learning together in a sort of sloppy unison, it seemed we were really quite good – an illusion that was shattered each time Nacho pointed at one of us to play alone, and it turned out that most of us really hadn't a clue.

The most confident-looking among the beginners was a Frenchman called Jean-Paul, who introduced himself as a professional musician. However, he refused to play on his own at all. 'I am a very timide personne,' he explained. 'I know zees stuff but I need to practise before I can play wiz zeez people.' Rather than rely on memory or observation, he chose to record the lessons on a very high-tech machine, to pore over once he got back to France. I had a listen to his recording of the first lesson – the one with my entrance – and it was hideous, the cacophony multiplied so that you couldn't make out a single useful phrase.

Strangely, Jean-Paul seemed to have a contempt for flamenco method and would repeatedly bring the lesson to a halt: 'But Nacho, zat ees a ridiculeuse way to make zat sound. Ees very more easy when you do eet like zis, non?' Then he would propose his own inept version. He kept this up all week. 'Wiz four fingeurs?! But zat ees clearly completely *impossible*, nobody can do zat wiz four fingeurs – neveure. It is bettaire to do eet wiz three, *comme ça...*'

Nacho maintained an admirable patience, explaining over and over again the techniques, while Jean-Paul would release an oath and with a Gallic shrug look round the rest of the class for support. But we were all with Nacho, and over the fortnight, most of us began to make real progress.

I certainly felt that I had improved, even though I was playing through the pain barrier, as the unaccustomed work gave me a hideous pain in the little muscles on the top of the finger, and my nails, worn thin by ceaseless playing, started to crack up.

At the end of the course, my nails actually required superglue to keep them in place. But I'd achieved what I came for. It was time to return to El Valero and impress the womenfolk.

Wwoofers

WOOF IS AN ACRONYM for 'Working Weekends On Organic Farms'. This concept started about thirty years ago, with the intention of helping struggling organic farmers with their labour-intensive endeavours, while also enabling city families with an interest in the countryside to get out there and into it, hoeing and weeding in the mud. The organisation has expanded and now, as *Willing Workers On Organic Farms*, provides a network of eccentric addresses to visit in almost any part of the globe. That's the *wwoof* hosts. The willing workers, or *wwoofers*, are a band of peripatetic young and not so young who are happy to exchange some labour for board and lodging in a beautiful landscape.

Part of the *wwoof* idea is that the farmers teach the *wwoofers* about organic farming but the reality is that the farmers often pick up as much as they share. Travelling from farm to farm the *wwoofers* are a valuable conduit of information for isolated and often uncommunicative farmers.

El Valero had obvious *wwoof* potential: a beautiful farm, whose owners had no spare cash for labour. So, over the years, we have taken on a string of *wwoofers*, most of them wonderful, though with the odd slob thrown in.

Gudrun and Jaime, our most recent *wwoofers*, were perhaps the most memorable of the lot.

Gudrun was a country girl from somewhere up in the turnip belt to the northwest of Berlin and had written us a pleasant and articulate letter asking if she could come and work on our farm for two or three weeks, as a volunteer. Then, a few days after receiving our invitation, she rang us to say she was on the way. I was dispatched to collect her from the bus stop.

A dozen or so people got off the bus that evening and dispersed into the dark streets, but none of them seemed to be Gudrun – not that I had any idea what she looked like. And then I spotted a lanky, blonde woman with a backpack trudging up the road. I strode after her.

'Would you be Gudrun?' I asked. She half turned and looked at me open-mouthed and baffled. We stared at one another in the gathering dark. The seconds moved towards a minute. Oh Lord, I thought. It's a bloke and he's not pleased to be confused with some Gudrun.

'Gudrun?' I said again weakly.

She looked at me a little longer. 'Oh,' she said.

'Hi, I'm Chris, good to meet you, how was your journey?' I said, assuming the 'oh' meant she was indeed Gudrun.

'Ohh,' she said again, with a slightly different inflection.

Maybe she's deaf, I thought, though she hadn't mentioned that in the letter. I took her pack and she followed me meekly down to the car.

On the journey home I tried my best to engage Gudrun in conversation, enunciating everything with the most precise elocution. But it soon became clear that the problem wasn't deafness at all. Gudrun spoke not a word of Spanish and barely any English – and I had a sneaking feeling that even in German she might not be a very communicative person. Not that I could tell, exactly, as my schoolboy German barely counted as human communication. *'Heute machen wir einen Ausflug nach Boppard* – Today we are going on an excursion to Boppard,' was about all I could muster, and it got us nowhere.

On arrival home Gudrun gave Ana a warm smile and disappeared to her room without a drink or a meal or anything. Ana and I stood looking at each other, wondering. 'Maybe she'll improve,' suggested Ana.

'Well, I certainly hope so. She's not going to be a ball of fun unless she does!' I said.

Next day, after a rather morose communal breakfast, Ana somehow managed to get the idea across to Gudrun that she wanted the vegetable patch weeded. Gudrun duly disappeared for the rest of the morning, and weeded the vegetable patch like a whirlwind. She was certainly one hell of a weeder. Ana made her coffee and they drank it together and smoked cigarettes, and in some indefinable non-verbal way they began to bond.

Perhaps as a result of Ana's prompting, Gudrun seemed to find me an amusing specimen, and would snigger whenever I came near her. I would smile blankly back, and little by little a limited relationship was established, aided by Gudrun's 'Ohs' and my occasional resurrection of the Boppard travel plans.

It may have been the infantile speech we were reduced to, but Gudrun seemed much younger than her twenty-five years. She was tall and etiolated in the way that adolescents look after a sudden growth spurt, and she had thick blonde hair that fell on either side of her face, framing a surprisingly broad smile. Little by little we came to like Gudrun, and as she began to feel more comfortable with us, she warmed and blossomed a little, and we saw more of the smiles. So Gudrun stayed on, sleeping in a storeroom that had been turned into a bedroom, and weeding and weeding.

Jaime was a very different kind of *wwoofer*: a young urban Spaniard from Madrid. When he first arrived amongst us he strode up to Manolo, who is still a long way from being modern and urban, gripped him in a firm handshake and, looking straight and clear into his eyes, said 'Hi, I'm Jaime.' Manolo looked forlornly at Ana for help.

Jaime was equally direct with the rest of us, addressing anyone he met, colloquially, in their own language. He was completely fluent in English, which he spoke with a trans-atlantic accent, picked up from a string of English-speaking girlfriends that stretched from Goa to Marin County. He was forever expanding his vocabulary, asking us questions that seriously taxed our knowledge of our own language. His main failing was that he couldn't bear to be wrong – and most particularly to be shown up as wrong, especially by a woman.

One day Ana and Jaime were looking at the dog kennel, which is a sort of nondescript brownish red. 'Tell me, Ana,' began Jaime. 'What's that colour in English? In Spanish it's *granate*.'

'Well, it's a sort of reddish brown, not really a colour at all,' she answered.

'Yeah, but what's the name of it?'

'Doesn't have a name.'

'C'mon, you can't be serious, man, that's a specific colour.'

'No it isn't, it's brownish. And if there is a name for it then I don't know it.' Ana was rising to the argument.

'Look, man... in Spanish it's *granate*. Everybody knows that. There's not a person in the whole goddam length and breadth of Spain who doesn't know what that colour is.'

Jaime was beginning to get agitated and at just that moment there came a 'mcep' sound from the *chumbo* and Manolo appeared with Porca on his shoulder. Porca likes Manolo.

'Look, now you'll see,' Jaime began to shout. 'I'll ask Manolo what colour it is... Hey Manolo, what colour is the dog kennel?'

Manolo looked uncertainly from Jaime to the dog kennel and back.

'Go on, tell us. What colour is it?'

'Well, it's a sort of reddish brown... isn't it?'

'No, man! You know perfectly well what colour it is! C'mon man, give me a break.'

'Then it's brown.'

'Jesus man! You know that colour. It's *granate*, isn't it.'

'*Granate*,' murmured Manolo, toying with the word.

'There, see, Ana, he said it. Everyone knows that word...'

Jaime prides himself upon his disciplined state of being, so it's always fun to see if you can get him riled up and knock him off the perch of his karma. He does a lot of work on it – tai chi and meditation, mainly – and, it has to be admitted, manages to achieve a fair degree of self-control.

In the evenings the rest of us would tend to slouch around on the sofa with a glass of wine or cup of chocolate, languorously talking, reading and listening to music by the fire. Jaime would arrive late, having completed his gruelling spiritual and physical workout sessions, offer everyone a polite good evening, then take his brick (he carries a wooden brick around with him) and plant it on the floor in the middle of the room. Lowering himself onto his brick he'd assume a half-lotus position with back ramrod straight. He would refuse a glass of wine but accept a glass of water for later, and there he would sit, speaking when spoken to, but otherwise staring fixedly at the flames of the fire, chanting mantras – quietly so as not to upset anybody. Needless to say, it drove us to distraction.

Sex was something that Jaime also claimed to be in control of. He was thirty-three and a very good-looking young man, with an Adonis-like physique – the result, so he told me, of rigorous physical workouts in his youth – and he had a philosophical approach to the temptations of the flesh. 'Well, of course I'm just a human being like everyone else and once in a while I need a woman,' he confided. 'Who doesn't? But you know, man, when you need a thing it very often comes along. The rest of the time I learn to live without it. If you don't... well, sex is a destructive force and it can throw you right out of your chosen path.'

One night, I drove Jaime and Gudrun to a Celtic music night in a bar in the hills. I found myself a comfy spot at the bar while Jaime took his brick and sat squarely in front of the band refusing any offer of a beer. Gudrun, meanwhile, moved around the crowd at the back, grooving to the music. They ignored one another altogether until in the back of the car on the way home, by sundry gropings, Gudrun made her intentions clear.

Next morning, while Gudrun sat outside on the terrace smoking her breakfast cigarette, Jaime sat down to breakfast with us. 'Jesus, she's a real tiger in bed, man!' he observed. I raised my eyebrows at Ana. We had already noticed Gudrun's air and had been indulging in an enjoyable sotto voce debate about which were the absolutely certain signs of passion, and which were incidental. For instance, was rubbing your neck more certain than smirking at the muesli?

Jaime, though, was not one for such subtleties. 'I'm goin' to need a whole lot of condoms, man,' he announced. 'Ana – when you go into town can you get me some condoms? Five packs ought to do.' Then he added, musing smugly to himself, 'God, what a body! It's just perfection, man... hey, make that ten packs, will you?'

Ana and I both went to town the next day. I remembered the condoms, and our wwoofers' relationship bloomed, with Jaime regaling us with frequent and explicit accounts of their doings. Romantic it was not. In fact, Jaime seemed to regard the arrangement mainly as a practical expedient for storing up some sex, camel-like, for the next lean period: 'She knows, man, because I told her, that this is definitely a relationship with an expiry date.'

Of course it was rather difficult to elicit from Gudrun how she felt about it but I sort of resented Jaime's coolness. I didn't think for a minute that Gudrun was a poor suffering dupe; she had instigated the relationship in the first place and had managed to get across to Ana that she treated it as no more than a holiday fling. But I like to see a bit of warmth and vulnerability between young lovers, and apart from the fact that we were always tripping over them snogging or groping one another, neither of them seemed to evince much tenderness. I wanted to see Jaime torn on the rack of passion. It was for his own good.

At the time I knew Jaime, he seemed like a water-boatman, flitting about on the surface of the deep pool of life. I felt he needed to be more like those silvery bottom-feeders that glide among the depths. From the surface of the water you can't see the bottom, only the sky reflected. And that's a pretty false impression to rely on.

Whatever my misgivings about Jaime and Gudrun's emotional life, they made a terrific gardening team. Gudrun seemed utterly in sympathy with Ana's horticultural aspirations and they just had to exchange a few vowel sounds over breakfast and Gudrun would know exactly what to do. Jaime, meanwhile, was engaged in the construction of a new path that would wind down from the house to the vegetable patch across a tiny rivulet of water that occasionally swelled to a stream.

In Gudrun's hands the plants were safe, while Jaime had designed a path and a little bridge of bound logs that was zen-like in its beauty. Jaime was an imaginative artist; whatever task he took on would be transformed into a creative masterpiece. Of course this wasn't always entirely convenient. Once the latch broke on our front door and he offered to replace it. After three days of having our home open and vulnerable to the elements and ravening beasts we were presented with one of the most beautifully shaped and engineered latches ever to grace a front door. Even now I feel guilty if I use it too roughly, as if at any moment it will be recalled to its rightful place in a gallery.

Sometimes Jaime joined us for meals, but usually he catered for himself. He was no great cook but knew, he insisted, exactly the necessary intake of calories per day that would keep him in good shape. At the beginning of the week he prepared a big saucepan of vegetable slop into which he put just about everything he could lay his hands on. He would heat this up daily and serve himself two ladlefuls for supper. He calculated it to last a whole week so he only had to cook once in that time.

It has to be said that Jaime was in remarkably good shape. Throughout the summer months he wandered about clad in the most minuscule of shorts so he could get a good even tan. He carried not an ounce of spare fat and had the muscular tone extremely well developed – tight belly-muscles with not a hint of flab, broad well-defined pectorals, good-looking meaty biceps, triceps, quadriceps, the whole bit.

Manolo, perhaps due to his keen appreciation of the fruits of the pig, is not quite as slender as he might be, although his ample layer of padding conceals an almost superhuman strength that Jaime could never hope to match. However, that summer Manolo gave Jaime's physique some consideration. For the first time ever we saw Manolo without his shirt on – that is something almost no true Alpujarran does. Manolo also considered the food that Jaime brought down to eat in the shade of the fig tree, and after a certain amount of discussion with Jaime about diet and its effect upon the physique, his packed lunch began to change. Vegetables, salads and fruit began to make an appearance and the immense slabs of *tocino* – pig fat – and stews played a less prominent part. Manolo figured that a modification of the physique might also have a beneficial effect upon his love-life, which was going through something of a lean period.

'It's a pity, you know, that Gudrun fancies me,' Jaime announced one morning, 'because she'd be just the girl for Manolo. I've told him that he's welcome to ask her. I'm not at all possessive.' Manolo was standing a few steps behind, smiling good-humouredly at his new mentor.

'That's generous of you, Jaime,' I answered, 'but don't you think Gudrun might have a say in this?'

Manolo, for his part, had a daring scheme he wanted to float with Gudrun. His elderly mother had been laid up at home following a knee operation and he thought Gudrun might like to extend her stay in the valley and take a job as lady's companion.

'Come on, Manolo,' I tried to bring him down to earth. 'Gudrun doesn't speak a word of Spanish! What the hell are she and your mother going to do together all day?' The thought defied imagination.

Manolo pondered this a moment.

'They can watch television,' he answered brightly.

I still couldn't see it working but Jaime pronounced it a great idea and said he would put it to Gudrun that very night.

Fortunately for all concerned that was the last we heard of it. Indeed, a few weeks later, Gudrun returned to Germany to embark on a nursing course.

If Manolo and Jaime were upset by her departure, then they hid it well, or perhaps I simply didn't notice the obvious signs. Throughout the spring that gradually unfolded, something new cropped up that, for a while, absorbed me utterly. I had an eco folly to build.

An Eco Folly

THE ORIGINS OF OUR ECO FOLLY can be dated to an early spring morning when I took the dogs for a walk up on the hillside behind the house. I noticed the slight figure of a man, high above me, picking his way down through the scrub. He stopped and began waving and jabbing an arm in the direction of the gorge as if he wanted me to look at something, but I couldn't make out what it might be. It was one of those days with barely a whisper of wind and only the odd *tutubía* dipping its way across a cloudless sky. Then I saw it: a surge of water was rolling down the Cádiar river, roaring as it came. Within minutes the whole riverbed was a pinkish-brown flood, dotted with clumps of bushes and trees that had been torn from the hills. Then, almost as soon as it had begun, the torrent subsided and the river returned to its normal steady sussuration.

I had heard about the awesome erosion of flash floods before but had never seen it in action. There must have been a violent and sudden rainstorm up in the hills of the Contraviesa, as the river was coloured by the red earth washed off its steep slopes. The water had been so thick with earth and sand that it had moved almost in slow motion, like a river of treacle, rearranging the topography of our riverbed.

I turned to look up the hill and saw the man who had been waving, approaching along the path. He was wearing a purple tracksuit and hopped over the stones with an agility that seemed at odds with his mop of curly grey hair. I noticed that he was carrying a stylish-looking retractable umbrella.

'Hallo,' the man said in English.

'Hallo,' I replied, looking with curiosity at the umbrella.

'Oh yes, it's a Japanese design, very compact...' he offered, marking my interest. 'I had an idea a storm might break, but I hadn't expected it to happen so far up.' And he talked at length about the phenomenon of flash-flooding, pointing out just why he thought the river had taken the course that it had.

I was fascinated by this display of hydrographical knowl-ege and stood there, nodding and putting in the odd question. 'Where are you going?' I asked eventually.

'I'm going back to my van. I've parked it about two kilo-metres up river – beyond that *cortijo* there,' and he pointed towards El Valero. 'It's Chris and Ana's place, if you know them..?'

'I do, I do...indeed I am them, or one of them.'

'Really? That's most felicitous,' he paused, savouring the word. 'I'd been intending to come over and introduce myself to you.'

'Felicitous indeed,' I said. 'Who are you, then?'

'I'm Trev,' he said, extending his hand. 'Not Trevor. Trev.'

I said I was pleased to meet him and suggested we walk back to the farm together. I was anxious to see what damage the flood had done to the river terrace. As we walked, Trev told me about his work as an itinerant ecological engineer and how he thought it possible that we might be in need of his services. I told him I wasn't sure exactly what an ecological engineer did – but if he could help me improve the efficiency of my solar power panels or improve on the shaky functioning of the *chumbo* – well, we could certainly use some help. Trev nodded at this but said that he preferred to put his mind to something more concrete – metaphorically speaking, he added hastily. He'd tell me what was possible when we'd had a look over the land.

We stopped at the house, where I made Trev a cup of herbal tea. When I carried it out onto the patio, I saw that he had walked down to the terrace by Ana's vegetable patch and was pacing slowly to and fro. Every now and again he would stop, look up at the sun and rub the side of his nose with his index finger; this, it appeared, was his preferred mode of thinking. Porca, who likes to keep an eye on his territory, was flitting between the branches of a large fig tree and studying the intruder.

'I've had a good look at your solar panels and your water systems,' Trev announced as I joined him. 'And I can see what you mean about the *chumbo*. It's a bit honky down there, isn't it? What you need is a reed-bed to clean up your waste.' Then, reaching out for his cup, he peered up into the branches of the fig: 'Ah – a Quaker Parakeet, I do like those,' he said, before resuming his flow. 'I reckon we're going to have to think laterally about fusing alternative and traditional technology in this place. It's a great spot to do it, mind – really very promising for the right sort of project.'

'Yes, you're right,' I said slowly. I noticed how he had said *we* and indeed this seemed like good innovative talk. 'So what eco-scheme do you think we should go for?'

'Well, it won't be easy and it won't be cheap, but I could help you build something bold and experimental – something that would really enhance as well as interact with the environment. If you're interested, of course.'

'Sounds interesting,' I said. 'So, what is it?!'

'A swimming pool,' he replied.

I looked at Trev incredulously.

'Are you crazy?' I said. 'What in hell would I want with one of those? If I want to swim, I can swim in the river, for Heaven's sake.'

He met my gaze with a quizzical look. 'That's not such a great prospect today,' he said, indicating with a nod of his head the devastation in the riverbed below.

It was true. The flood and its sludge had carried away all trace of our swimming-hole, created with a bit of tractor-shovelling from Manolo and a precarious dam of boulders. It would take a long, hot day's work to collect the boulders for another.

Trev folded an arm across his stomach, rested the other elbow in the cup of his hand and resumed fondling his nose. 'I think maybe there's a bit of confusion as to what I mean by the term swimming pool.'

It turned out that 'swimming pool' was in fact entirely the wrong term for the concept Trev had in mind for El Valero. 'I'm not thinking of digging a rectangular hole in the ground...' he explained, '...painting it turquoise and filling it full of chemicals. Oh no, I'm not into that at all. I'm thinking of bringing water closer to your home, creating an eco-sphere – one that you can swim in, mind – that will be natural and clean and yet not have a drop of chlorine in it.'

And Trev went on to explain why chlorine was the very bane of the planet; how aerosols and fridges and bovine flatulence were good for the ozone layer compared to what the chlorine in people's swimming pools was doing. Then he began to sketch the idea that he had been developing for just such a client as myself, who appreciated ecology, who treated his farm and landscape as a kind of garden, who had notions about leaving the earth enriched rather than denuded and impoverished.

There was a real beauty about Trev's ideas and it all sounded a long way from swimming pool salesmanship. He imagined our eco-sphere (for swimming) as a pool of crystalline water, filtered by secondary pools filled with a cleansing jungle of lilies, reeds, rushes and water-mints. Schools of delicious fish, later to be harvested for the household, would cruise to and fro devouring the organisms and micro-organisms inimical to the purity of our pond. A great bolster of raw untreated sheep's wool would float upon the surface of the reed-pool to suck up all the gunk that fouled the water from sunburn oil and other unguents. And any organism or clod of muck that escaped this formidable net was to be lofted by a solar-powered waterwheel up to an immense stone bottle filled with selected sands and sifted earths from long before the dawn of man. (You could buy this stuff, apparently, in bags from swimming pool shops.)

From the great bottle the filtered water would meander along stone runnels where the action of the sun's rays upon the thinly spread flow would knock any surviving bacteria on the head. Then the pure water would cascade over a fall of sun-baked stones back into the main pool. The whole was to be constructed using natural and locally-occurring materials; the shapes were to be organic and uplifting; the landscaping with stone and plants indigenous and exotic; and the project could be completed with an unpretentious pavilion of pisé and thatch.

It was clearly a mad, ludicrously complex scheme, and one based on a whole rake of optimistic assumptions. No one in their right mind would ever commision such a project.

I engaged Trev and his scheme on the spot.

I whiled away the rest of the morning in vainglorious thoughts of El Valero as a showpiece of eco-technology. Sitting on the terrace beside the vegetable patch – an auspicious spot according to Trev – I pictured Ana, Chloë and me floating happily among the lilies and gazing out across the mountains and rivers, while carp darted in the depths beneath.

My pleasant daydream was dispelled by the hoot of the car and the sound of dogs barking. Ana and Chloë were back from Orgiva. Jaime and Manolo had also come up to the house to collect some tools, and we all sat down on the terrace to have a drink in the shade. I could hardly contain myself and burst at once into an account of the flood, my meeting with Trev, and our bold new plans for reshaping the landscape of El Valero.

Chloë was thrilled. 'Our very own swimming pool,' she cheered, hopping around in excitement and setting the dogs off again. Bathing in the river, apparently, held no great charm for an eight-year-old. She pointed out that it wasn't easy to practise your strokes on a sludgy river bottom with water barely reaching the top of your knees, and as the riverbed is quite wide, it means you get hot and dusty again before you've made it back to your towel hanging in the willow tree, let alone the house. Her only concern about Trev's eco-scheme was whether the pool would be ready in time for her friend Hannah's visit the next weekend.

Ana, once she'd digested the fact that I was serious about the project, and had indeed good as commissioned it, was also inclined to be positive, particularly about its botanical aspect. 'It does sound beautiful,' she conceded, 'and I've always liked the idea of El Valero having its own grand folly. But how do you know it will work? You seem to be taking an awful lot on trust. And what do you actually know about this man Trevor and his earthly works?'

I had to concede that I didn't know much. Trev and I had talked a little that morning about his previous projects and his chosen life. He had, for the past five years, been dividing his time between England, the Pyrenees and the Alpujarras, moving from one to the other in a customised van-cum-home-cum-office, stopping for however long a project involved. For the last couple of months he had been working at *Cortijo Romero*, an alternative therapy centre just outside Orgiva. The centre specialised in personal development courses, rebirthing, yoga, circle-dances and the like. Trev had designed and installed a complex underfloor heating system for the therapy rooms. 'And what could be more important?' I asked rhetorically, 'if you're casting off the shackles of your hidebound ego, than a nice, warm floor to do it on?'

Ana seemed to agree but said she'd be keen to hear how the system worked when winter arrived and it was actually switched on. However, Jaime was straightforwardly enthusiastic. He seemed to understand the workings of the project better than any of us and was keen to see how it all pieced together. 'I doubt I'll be here to take a dip in it, though, man,' he said. 'This is going to be a tricky project to get right; it could take months.'

Manolo, who'd been smiling to himself throughout these discussions, looked stunned. 'Months?' he spluttered. 'It's only a swimming pool.' Manolo had orthodox views about how pools were built, having worked on a few in his time. The one unassailable rule was that they took no longer than six weeks. More than that and the workmen were either incompetent or robbing you blind, or both.

I explained yet again how this was going to be very different from your average chemical pool, and that we were going to create a whole new eco-sphere with cunning contrivances to keep the water clean and pure.

Manolo heard me out and then, resuming his habitual smile, asked: 'So, no chlorine, then?'

'No, Manolo,' I answered. 'No chlorine.'

Over the next fortnight, Trev hurled himself into calculations, diagrams and settings like a man possessed. The floodgates that had too often held back his visionary schemes now opened wide under our patronage, and the ideas came bursting forth. He lived the project, breathed it, slept it, drank it and ate it. The eating took the form of odd bits of greenery stuffed artlessly into a wholemeal bun: an odd diet that turned out to be an attempt to regain the affections of his girlfriend. She had, apparently, given him the boot (by email), because what she was after was a full-blooded vegan partner, and Trev's half-baked vegetarianism fell way below the mark. We knew there was some justice in this, as when Trev came to eat with us he would hunker down to a plate of roast chicken like a proper trencher-man.

From time to time, in order to see computer projections of the project, I would pay a visit to Trev's van. This was parked in the shade of an olive tree on the far side of the river. From the outside it looked ordinary enough, the sort of van you might hire to load up a market stall, except that it had two large solar panels propped beside it on a rock, with a cord trailing back into the engine. On sunny days these panels provided more than enough electricity to run his computer and domestic appliances and on dull ones he could always charge up his solar batteries with a drive. He had also managed to find the nearest spot to El Valero where you could use a mobile phone and I would often come across him sitting on the hill with his laptop, surfing the Internet.

The only thing at odds with this technological Tardis were the van doors. When Trev first told me they were diffi-cult to open, indicating that I should stand back while he did so, I assumed they must work on some state of the art time-lock device. In fact, they were dented and just needed to be kicked hard in a particular spot and then wrestled open with the handle. It was nice to see an old-fashioned method enduring.

Trev seemed able to turn his hand to almost any mechanical or electronic task, forging solutions with a mixture of science, art and Heath Robinson make-do. As the ecosphere project took shape, he adapted the windscreen-wiper-motor out of our old Land Rover and fitted it up to drive a bank of solar panels that moved with the progress of the sun, lying perpendicular to the sun's rays all day and winding back at night to the starting position. The capacity of the panels was calculated to drive another motor – lifted from a defunct cement-mixer – that turns the waterwheel, whose lifting capacity is calculated in turn to move the entire volume of water of the pool three times through the filter, using the twelve hours of sunshine that we enjoy on an average summer day.

Throughout proceedings, the aesthetic consideration remained paramount, not least because Trev is also an artist. He shows his art works under the name of Val Dolphin (which has rather more pull in Bohemian circles than Trevor Miller) though the art is apparent in everything he designs. His pool steps, for example, sweep down in a spiral that calls to mind the interlocking leaves inside the aperture of a lens or that masterpiece of Bauhaus aquatic sculpture, the Penguin Pool at London Zoo.

All of this was exactly as I would have had it, except for one small failing – a failing that threatened to engulf our grand endeavour in a fog of rancour. Trev was an absolute perfectionist. He had no toleration whatsoever of errors and viewed even tiny deviations from his plans as jeopardising the entire project. Quite possibly he was right. But it was hard on both the soul and coffers to pull work apart and start all over again because a step, say, was two centimetres out, or the materials were discovered to be not quite up to scratch.

There was also the problem of lost days where we did nothing but wait for new parts to be sourced or materials to arrive, leaving Manolo, Jaime and me to do sporadic stints of labour when the right materials were to hand. And then with summer just around the corner and no swimming pool in sight, I cracked. Manolo and I had been working hard on completing the weir that separated the fish pond and sump. The sump was where the water was gathered for lifting by the waterwheel into the sand filter. For a whole day we'd struggled to get the levels right. It was slow, back-breaking work but we kept at it, knowing that the end was at last in sight and we could soon move on to another task. Then Trev appeared on the scene in his neatly laundered, off-white overalls, watched for a while and shook his head.

'No, no, that won't do at all,' he called. 'That's way off.'

'What do you mean?' I spluttered.

'It's way off. It's not level. You can see it's not level, even from here. I'm afraid you'll have to do it again.'

Manolo shrugged but I was ready for battle. 'Now look here, Trev,' I said. 'What the hell does it matter if it's a tiny smidgeon out? It's only a pool for heaven's sake – it's not the bloody Hanging Gardens of Babylon.'

Trev wheeled round as if stung.

'Alright. If you want to botch it up, then just say. It's your money and you do what you want with it. Me, I want to do a good job and create a thing of real beauty. You think about it, Chris. You give it some good, hard thought.' And with that he stomped off the site in the direction of his van, one finger rubbing hard at the side of his nose.

Deflated, I sat on a rock. Of course, Trev was being too finickity, but this was no way to handle things. I looked round at Manolo and Jaime but instead of backing my outburst, they both looked as if they thought I was in the wrong and had made a mess of it.

At lunch, I talked it over with Ana.

'You've got this far,' she said, 'You might as well finish the thing off properly. It's a pity to spoil the ship for a ha'porth of tar.'

'Yes, I know. You're right.'

That afternoon I strode down to the site and set to with a sledgehammer, demolishing our weir. Trev reappeared towards the end of the day.

'So we're going for the thing of beauty,' he confirmed, looking at my pile of rubble.

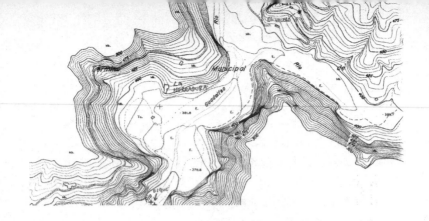

THE MEN IN TWEEDS

GOOD ANTIDOTE TO THE COMPLEXITY of existence is to go and start up a tractor. Taking advantage of Manolo's absence one weekend, I decided to go down and do a little tractor work. I began by cultivating the field below the stable, a piece of land that hadn't been turned over for years.

The effect of watering and the hammering of the sheep's hooves had made the surface like concrete. I had to pile rocks on the cultivator to make any impression on the soil, and even then it just broke into thick grey clods. After a few passes, though, a fine sweet-smelling tilth began to appear, and the work became a pleasure. At the bottom of the field is a line of lemon trees and each time I passed beneath them the tractor's smokestack would shoot up and a shower of pale petals would fall on the tractor and me, and cover the earth with a mosaic of creamy white.

The chugging of the tractor, the soil furling over the cultivator shares, and the quiet flurries of petals, induced in me a sort of trance. Agriculture can be beautiful, I mused. I looked round at the terraces of carefully pruned orange trees, the anarchic tangle of vines over by the stable, and the alfalfa thickening up for the first cut, and allowed myself a satisfied sigh. It's true that I wasn't the most proficient farmer and that despite years of hard, sometimes back-breaking work, we were no nearer to earning a living wage from the farm. But there are other ways to profit: for one, there is the privilege of enriching our own environment – a tiny patch of the earth, green as an oasis and framed by mountains, rivers and a clear canopy of sky.

My mind drifted along, a little complacently perhaps, thinking about all the stones we had picked out of the fields, about the soil itself – which, each time I dug it over, seemed a little richer, a little darker, heaving just a bit more with bacteria. Life seemed pretty good. And then my reverie was broken by a loud whoop from Ana, up at the house. She was waving from the terrace, having just got back from town.

I whooped back, to signal I was coming up, and watched her walk slowly back towards the kitchen. Even from that distance, half-masked in a mass of excitable dogs, I could tell something was up. I stopped the tractor and set off for the house.

Ana had a letter to show me, a formal one in an official-looking envelope that she had picked up from the post office. It was from the *Confederación Hidrográfica* – the River Authority – and it stated, as simply as governmental language will allow, that because the *acequia* that belongs to our farm was not officially registered, the *Confederación* would not be able to offer us any protection if it were disputed in any way. As no one had shown the slightest interest in disputing our *acequia* – our source of irrigation for the farm – this struck us as ominous. The letter ended by inviting us, should we require any clarification or assistance, to visit the *Confederación* in its lair in Malaga. It was signed by one Juan-Manuel Baldomero.

I looked at Ana. It was clear this boded badly, but I couldn't quite say why or how. Ana, who is rather more adept at deciphering coded threats, was equally puzzled. 'It's very odd,' she pondered. 'I thought maybe this was to do with reviving the hydroelectric scheme, but then why didn't they send it when the project was first mooted? I can't help wondering if they're preparing the ground for something even worse.'

Ana was referring to plans that had been around for a while to build a hydroelectric generating station upriver from our farm. This would have involved drilling through several kilometres of mountain to divert the river. It would fill the valley with heaps of debris, jeopardise all our water supplies, and create a potential health hazard from high voltage power-lines. The plans, though, seemed to have been shelved over a year ago. It made no sense that they should need to dispute our *acequia* to revive them now. I looked around for the envelope in case it might hold a clue. But it was gone. Porca, on the basis that Ana's enemy was his own, had removed the offensive article and was busy shredding it from his fastness on the shower taps.

Two days later Ana and I set off to Malaga to see Juan-Manuel Baldomero. The headquarters of the *Confederación Hidrográfica* was an unprepossessing red-brick building, near the city's botanical gardens. We ventured inside, trying not to look too apprehensive. Of course Señor Baldomero was not there; he was apparently having a morning coffee. But we could wait for him, they said. We sat on a couple of wooden chairs in a corridor outside his grand and spacious office.

The door was open, so we could easily verify the truth of the fact that he was indeed not there. Meanwhile, people wandered past us, with huge sheaves of papers and files, and occasionally a crisply dressed man or woman would stop and politely ask us what we were doing there. 'We're waiting for Juan-Manuel Baldomero,' we would answer – 'He's having coffee.' '*Claro* – of course,' they'd reply. 'He would be having coffee at this time of the morning.' And they would go on their way.

Ana and I chatted in desultory whispers, the way you do waiting for a headmaster or a hospital consultant. More people stopped and expressed an interest in what we were doing there. We would show them the letter. They would pore over it with an expression of concentration, then hand it back saying: 'You need to see Juan-Manuel Baldomero about that.' 'That's right,' we'd concur – 'He's having coffee.' 'So he is, so he is.'

As the morning ran its course, we started to get to know the inhabitants of the *Confederación* pretty well. An awful lot of their work seemed to consist in carrying sheaves of paper from one office to another. Still, they were friendly enough folk, and when they had seen us for the umpteenth time, they just smiled at us, having run out of things to say.

After a long time a very important-looking character in a tweed jacket and a tie came round the corner. 'At last,' we said to each other. 'This'll be Juan-Manuel Baldomero.'

We stood up, shook hands, introduced ourselves and showed him the letter, which he scanned with a rather exaggerated air of concentration. Then he looked at us over the top of his glasses and read it again, and finally, with his head still buried beneath the letter, he ushered us into the office. We sat down on straight wooden chairs opposite the desk.

'Well, then...' he said, whisking his glasses off. 'You'll need to see Juan-Manuel Baldomero about this.'

'Yes, but he's having his coffee,' we replied.

'Indeed he is,' said our new friend. 'Still, you might as well wait in the office. It's more comfortable and, while you're at it, you can cast your eye over this lot.' He fished about on the desk and pushed across a green file, as thick as a brick on its side.

'But what will Juan-Manuel Baldomero say when he finds two strangers sitting at his desk leafing about in his files?' I asked.

'Oh, he won't mind a bit. I'll see if I can find him for you,' he said, and disappeared up the corridor, leaving us alone in the office with the file.

By now, there was about an hour left before the office would close for lunch, so Ana and I set urgently to rooting about in the file, pleased to be down to business at last.

Most of the contents were complete gobbledegook: reams of administrative memos, pages of graphs and tables and pie-charts, heaps of letters from one 'most excellent body' to another, heaving with respectful esteem and couched in the most impenetrable jargon. It takes a certain sort of person, well versed in the arts of administration to flick quickly through such a pile without getting swamped. Within minutes my eyes were glazing over. Ana, though, who has some nebulous qualification in business studies, seemed rather better at it.

'What are we actually after?' I asked her, setting down my half of the file papers.

'Anything at all about El Valero, the rivers and the hydroelectric scheme,' she whispered conspiratorially. 'The company that proposed it was called *Saltos de Sierra Nevada*.'

'Here's *Saltos de Sierra Nevada*,' I cried out, rather pleased to have stumbled so quickly upon it. There was a whole batch of papers about the project.

We pored eagerly over them, page after page of permissions and prognostications and measurements; and then, towards the back, we came across a page entitled *Acequia del Valero*. 'Fancy that,' I said to Ana. 'A whole page devoted to us!'

I shut up and we both read the page and looked at the drawing. It seemed to me that the *Saltos de Sierra Nevada* project was by no means shelved but that the company had instead backed down a bit and were scaling down the scheme. Ana and I sat back for a moment to digest the information.

I broke the silence. 'Well... it's bad but not dreadful, you know. The plant won't encroach so much on the river and it'll be less of an eyesore...' I trailed off.

Ana wasn't listening. She was studying the back of the page and her face had drained of colour.

'What is it, what's the matter?' I exclaimed.

She pushed the page in front of me. There was a drawing of a dam, with detailed elevations and map references. It was headed 'Proposed Retention Dam at El Cerrado del Granadino' and beneath the drawing was a letter saying that *Saltos de Sierra Nevada* would move their proposed hydroelectric station to allow for the rise in the riverbed occasioned by the construction of the new dam. They would not demand any indemnification from the water authority for this loss.

Ana had gone quiet. El Granadino is scarcely a kilometre downriver from us, and what we were looking at was a proposal for the damming of our valley: the very dam I had feared, ever since buying the farm. The proposal was specific. The dam was not about water or hydroelectricity. Its function was something altogether different; it was a filter to stop silt and boulders continuing down to the vast new barrage at Rules, near the coast. Rules was one of Spain's largest ever engineering works, with a span of 900 metres and a budget of 40,000 million pesetas.

We were a small detail in this great project but the paper in front of us mapped out our valley's role in the scheme. The Granadino filter dam was to be fifty metres high and porous, so ultimately the valley would be flooded not by water but by silt building up behind the dam. This would rise to the 425-metre contour line, marked in bold on the map. The hillock at the bottom of our farm was marked as 404 metres. We could lose the whole of El Valero.

As Ana and I looked at one another in disbelief, another important man in a tweed jacket and tie appeared in the doorway. He introduced himself to us as Juan-Manuel Baldomero.

'Ah, so you're looking at the *expediente* – the file,' he said. 'Have you found anything of interest to you?'

'Well, yes, as a matter of fact we have,' I replied.

He looked down at the file and rubbed his thumb through his moustache. 'Hmm, El Granadino – the retention dam.'

'It's just downriver from our farm,' I blurted out. 'At those heights it looks like it's going to bury our whole farm under silt. We need to know if this is going to happen – and if so, when.'

'You can imagine it matters a lot to us,' Ana added quietly.

Baldomero rubbed his moustache again. 'Well,' he enunciated carefully. 'You do speak Spanish, I take it?'

'We do,' we said.

At this moment, the man who had shown us into the office came in and moved across to join our group standing around the desk. He picked up the file and took a quick glance at the offending page. It was clearly a familiar sight.

'Well,' continued Baldomero. 'You must realise that at the moment this is no more than a possibility. None of the permissions have been granted. There's nothing happening.' And he went on to explain that there were any number of hurdles at which a project of this magnitude might stumble, so it was a little premature to worry about farming under water or indeed silt.

It was a sympathetic speech and would have been extremely reassuring if we had been able to believe it. Ana had, by now, fixed her gaze on the first man with the tweed jacket. He seemed to understand that his opinion was also needed here and, in a slightly more succinct way, repeated his colleague's observations. 'Yes, it's true. There's nothing definite yet, and even in a worst case scenario – the very worst from your perspective – it would take many years for the river to dislodge enough silt to seriously threaten your land.'

'How many?' asked Ana.

Mr Tweed looked puzzled.

'Years,' she explained.

He shrugged and spread his hands. 'How can anyone say? The river is unreliable. Really, all we can do is keep you informed. And although, of course, I can't give you any guarantees, this scheme really shouldn't be a major worry for you.'

These repeated reassurances were becoming ever more disconcerting. 'Look...' I said, slightly more loudly than intended. Ana shot me a glance. 'Look – we've planned to live the rest of our lives on this farm. Do you recommend that we continue with this plan, that we plant trees, build things, invest our time and savings on it? We need to know.'

The two men looked at a survey map that Baldomero had opened on the desk. It was a very large-scale map with all the contour lines clearly marked.

'I'm not sure we're in a position to give a definite answer to that. There's too much uncertainty. We'll know a lot more about it in a year's time,' Baldomero answered.

'But if it were you, would you sink most of your savings into the place?' asked Ana looking directly at Mr Tweed.

There was a pause.

'No,' he answered. 'I don't think I would.'

Then it was lunchtime. Ana and I found a bar not far from the *Confederación* and settled down to take in the enormity of what we had just discovered. We ordered a bottle of wine and some sort of fish; Malaga's seafood is legendary, but we might as well have been chewing cold fish fingers. I took Ana's hand beneath the table and squeezed it and gave her a sad sort of smile.

'Oh well, it could be a lot worse!' I said.

'I knew you were going to say that,' she smiled thinly back.

'I knew you knew I was going to say it – that's why I said it. But you know what I think?' I added.

'No, tell me,' said Ana.

'Well, it's one hell of a big valley. It'll take a long time to fill up. My guess is that it would take an age to reach even the sheep shed. And by then you, me and maybe even Chloë will be too old to care. And so will the sheep.'

'Speak for yourself,' she muttered.

Still, we made a decision over that lunch. We would find out all we could about the dam project and, if necessary, we'd try to fight it. But we wouldn't drag each other and Chloë into despondency. We resolved there and then to be positive and the first positive step we'd take would be to consult the local environmental group.

And so saying, we walked briskly out of the restaurant talking animatedly and with great good humour about subjects that didn't interest us in the slightest.

DEFENDERS OF THE RIVER

OMINGO WAS THE FIRST PERSON we consulted about the dam proposal, but his reaction was a disappointment. Typical of rural Spaniards when faced with the might of the state, he was phlegmatic and fatalistic. 'Who can tell,' he shrugged. 'If they build their dam, perhaps it won't work, perhaps it will. But there's no stopping big projects. We country people count for nothing with the men in power.' This was the view in Tíjolas, too: you don't have a chance with authority. The next week, however, we ran into Gary, a carpenter friend from Capileira, who told us about the *Unión Verde Alpujarreña*, or 'Green Union,' of which he was a member. He suggested we take our information along for the group's consideration: we were pleased with this idea; it seemed like a good positive step.

But as it turned out, we never did get to address the UVA, for a few days later we met Gary again and he had a sorry tale. He had gone along to the monthly meeting intent on telling the group about the dam threat, and hoping to get a proposal of his own adopted – something simple for the group to get their teeth into. His proposal involved clearing the heaps of rubbish that had accumulated over the years around the spring by the village of Ferreirola. Gary figured this was an undertaking that ought just about to fall within the group's organisational abilities. When he arrived at the meeting, though, nursing his proposal, the group was already locked in impassioned debate. The issue on the agenda was a sweeping one: a world-wide ban on the production of plastics. After an hour or more of furious polemic, during which Gary tried several times, unsuccessfully, to table his proposal, the plastics motion was put to the vote.

'It was the first motion that was ever carried unanimously in the whole history of the group,' said Gary with a resigned grin. 'There was some doubt as to how they were going to implement it, but that was soon forgotten when the treasurer stood up to give account of the financial situation. The UVA were virtually without funds: in fact, there was only enough to buy the assembled company a round or two of drinks. So we voted to disband and adjourn to the bar, and again it was passed unanimously.'

'But where does that leave us?' we wondered.

'You could always try José-Luis and his *Colectivo Ecologista* in Tablones,' suggested Gary. 'They'd probably be a whole lot more effective than the UVA, anyway.'

The *Colectivo Ecologista*, Gary told us, were serious people. They would know how to get proper investigations underway, and José-Luis was a real force – not just a bar-radical. He was an activist to the core, a big bear of a man who earned his living teaching would-be plumbers in Albuñol, a town surrounded by a hideous sea of plastic greenhouses. He had moved down to the Alpujarras from Santander, in northern Spain, and even after five years' residence he was still considered an outsider by his neighbours. However, he devoted almost all his free time to local environmental issues, and had gained a reputation for exposing corrupt and illegal development schemes, and putting a spanner in their works. His weapons were a certain legal acumen, an ability to see through the obfuscations of bureaucracy, and a deafness to threats and backhanders.

No sooner had Gary instilled the idea of contacting José-Luis than I began to hear of him from all quarters. The *Colectivo* had, it seemed, quite a track record. The year before they had launched a protest against plans to build an asphalt factory at Tablones that would have poisoned the air and almost certainly contaminated the river if it had gone ahead. The plans were found to be illegal and had to be shelved. So too had the plans to exploit a nearby site for a quarry: the fear, this time, being that the dust would spread for miles over the farm land, choking trees and crops. José-Luis had discovered, among other irregularities, that the projected site was *Patrimonio de Juventud*, held in trust for the youth of the municipality, and thus couldn't be touched. He had aired this issue, among others, to the council, and the Mayor had called a halt.

It was with a deal of curiosity, and some hope, then, that I made my way on a sultry summer's evening to Tablones and out along the riverbed of the Guadalfeo, looking for José Luis's house. I had no very clear idea of the sort of place I expected an environmental activist to live in, but I was a little surprised to find the patio of his single-storey house surrounded by chicken wire (the previous owner, apparently, used it as a chicken run). Behind the wire a little girl was playing with some clothes pegs while her mother folded sheets. The front door was open and she gestured me inside with a friendly smile and wave, leaving me to follow a trail of cigarette smoke to a small windowless room that formed the HQ of *El Colectivo Ecologista y Cultural Guadalfeo*. Here, wedged between piles of books, ashtrays and affidavits, sat José-Luis, staring intently at a computer screen.

'*Hola*, welcome. You must be Cristóbal,' he said, wresting his attention from the screen long enough to shake my hand, flick a butt into the bin and run a newly rolled cigarette across his tongue. 'What do you think of this?'

Without further preamble he swung his massive frame back towards the screen and clicked on a picture, revealing a vast, yellow expanse of greenhouse plastic spreading across a series of fields down to the coast.

'Not very nice, is it?' he observed, 'especially for the labourers who have to live and breathe the foul concentrations of toxins all day. That's why they use Moroccan immigrants, you know. They can coerce them into staying, and no one's going to bother much about the respiratory problems they get.' And José-Luis launched into a catalogue of environmental and human damage wreaked by the greenhouse entrepreneurs, talking with passion about the tips of empty agro-chemical drums, the rocketing crime rate generated by this new business, and his fears that the dirty sea of plastic would soon start to encroach on the Alpujarras.

José-Luis seemed so engaged by this issue, and it seemed so fulsome a disaster, despite its boon to the local economy, that

I felt reluctant to divert his attention to a lesser problem, such as our threatened dam. But he had heard about our interview in Malaga and wanted to know everything about it.

'Well... perhaps you'll have a look at this,' I began apologetically, placing a piece of paper on the table beside his ashtray.

'What on earth is it?' he asked, peering closely at it through a fog of smoke. 'It looks to me like a design for an aquarium.'

It was in fact my sketch of the plan that we had seen in the file at the *Confederación Hidrográfica*.

'It's the dam.'

'Ah, so it is... and where exactly is it to be built?'

'Just upriver from us, by El Granadino.'

José-Luis blew away a bit of ash that had fallen on the sheet and studied it through narrowed eyes. 'Go on, then, tell me everything you know about it.'

So I told him what the dam was and how we had discovered it and what the tweed men had said about it.

José-Luis frowned. 'By the look of this, you and probably a few others are going to lose a sizeable part of your farms,' he said. 'And the whole eco-system of the valley will be screwed, good and proper.'

'That's right.'

'Well then, we'd better do something about it, hadn't we?'

In Andalucia, the preferred method for dealing with threats to the environment, or any other assault on the public interest, is to have a fiesta. This can achieve a number of

goals at once: it can raise money, it can build public aware-
ness of an issue, and, last but not least, everybody gets to
have a good time.

Once José-Luis was on the case, the *Colectivo* swung
swiftly into action. A fiesta committee was formed; posters with the date and venue were printed and distributed;
beer, wine and mountains of meat were ordered; and musicians, the sort willing to play for free, were booked. The
venue, perhaps, didn't have an altogether ecological ring
– Tablones cement-works – but it was the nearest thing to
a flat patch of land that Tablones could offer. The date was
a Saturday in mid-August.

The allotted night was starry and hot – it always is in
August. Ana sold tickets for the food and drink, while I
worked on the *pinchitos*, the kebab stall. The wine was not
of the best but, with the night heat stoking the barbecue
to an inferno, you drank whatever you could get. I drained
my paper cup again and again, keeping pace with Abu Bakr,
opposite, who was gulping mint tea at the halal *pinchitos*
stall set up for the Muslim contingent.

For my own *pinchitos*, I had prepared an exotic marinade of
ginger, garlic, onions, chillies, soy sauce, honey and sherry.
This wasn't as good as I had hoped, as I overdid the sherry,
with the result that the marinade didn't stick to the meat
at all. Also my pork cubes were too big, meaning that the
sweet wet meat was burned on the outside and raw in the
middle. Still, most of the diners were too drunk to notice.

First on, as darkness fell, was a Cuban band composed
of Spanish and Germans, with a French singer whose voice
put me in mind of Billie Holiday. Musically, they were as
good as the evening got, but they were near inaudible as
the *colectivista* in charge of the sound system hadn't yet

arrived. Still, the night was young and as midnight passed, the amplification cranked into action, and revellers arrived from all across the Alpujarras and from as far away as Motril and Granada.

José-Luis shouldered his way through the throng, grinning exultantly and greeting people with great thumps on the back, leaving a trail of spluttered pork and wine. 'There's a good thousand people here – maybe two!' he yelled, as a sudden burst of bass and drums announced the next act.

A thrash metal band had taken to the stage. They were José-Luis's plumbing students and strong candidates for the worst band in Andalucia. The lead singer leapt about the stage yelling indecipherable lyrics against a cacophony of white noise that became more painful by the minute. Even the Spanish hardcore, who could chat over a hurricane, seemed to be cowering away from the speaker stacks. But the band were so delighted to be playing that there seemed no way of ever getting them off. Then at last someone hit upon the idea of pulling the plug and a sigh of relief rose from the crowd.

Ana came across for a *pinchito*, with a big grin on her face. 'Good turn-out, isn't it?' she said. 'There must be at least five hundred here! It's an amazing start.'

My reply was cut off by a fearful screech and yowl of microphone feedback as José-Luis prepared to address the crowd.

'Friends and comrades!!' he yelled. 'You know why we're here tonight. We're here to save the Alpujarras.' A cheer went up from the revellers. 'We're here to save the Alpujarras from the sharks and from the vultures' – the cheer grew – 'from the speculators and the property developers, from the callous industrialists who are trying to destroy our mountains...'

José-Luis was good at this; he was a born orator and the crowd was already on his side. This being the Alpujarras, the bulk of it was made up of alternative lifestylers – anarchists, artists, healers, herbalists, meditators, vegans, ovo-lacto-vegetarians and the like – along with a sprinkling of skinheads and thugs, up for a Saturday night of thrash metal and kebabs. Still, there was a feeling of euphoria, and as José-Luis hunkered down into a harangue about the threats to the Alpujarran environment – the dam, the asphalt plant, the piping of the rivers – the crowd's rumblings became a roar and fists were raised in the air. It looked like the vultures and the sharks were well out of their league this time.

The crowd had been continuing to swell, and the demand for meat had long overtaken supply – even my oriental-style kebabs were getting wolfed down – while the wine, the beer and the *Cuba Libres* poured across the counters in ever more gargantuan quantities. Through the meat smoke, I smiled a slightly stupefied smile at Ana. I was just the tiniest bit fuddled with wine, but things were looking good and we were all having a hell of a good time. A local reggae band were doing their stuff, and their flashing lights illuminated the clouds of dust billowing from the dancers' feet. I weaved unsteadily through the crowd and whirled Ana away in a dipping, hopping, arm-waving stumble of a dance.

After the bills had been paid, the fiesta actually turned a modest profit, and the *Colectivo* set about spending it, producing pamphlets and posters, featuring the slogan *Acequias SI! Dique NO!* – 'Irrigation-canals YES! Dyke NO!'

Well, it sounded okay in the Spanish, and the activists made sure that every tree, sign and building throughout the Alpujarras proclaimed their message.

Meetings were also held to raise the consciousness of those unable to benefit from the fiesta. In remote villages across the Alpujarras, tiny gaggles of locals would gather beneath the poplars and chestnuts to hear José-Luis describe the environmental threats facing the region. I'd like to say that they were whipped up into a frenzy of defiance and immediately pledged their support but most often they seemed indifferent to matters far from their own farms and grazing.

Inevitably, perhaps, our optimism began to wane and as autumn turned to winter, the campaign against the dam began gradually to lose its momentum. For a few weeks, hope was rekindled when a specialist lawyer agreed to look into the case, but he proved unable to find a legal challenge that he thought would stick. His opinion was that we might hold up proceedings for short periods, at great cost and, possibly, some personal risk, but he doubted we could ever bring the dam to an effective halt.

Ana, who had become an avid reader of *El Ecologista*, the magazine of the Spanish Ecology movement, had been following the progress of a similar dam being built at Itoiz, in Navarra. It presented a salutary picture. Apparently, the opposition to this huge and unpopular project had strong European support and had won all the necessary legal battles to get the dam shelved. But the State decided to sweep aside the legal challenges and go ahead with it anyway – while handing out stiff prison sentences to many of the eco-activists involved. It was depressing to discover that Domingo had grounds for his pessimism. The State seemed, indeed, to do as it pleased.

José-Luis didn't try to hide his disappointment when I told him that I thought we should stop battling on with a project that had no chance of success. Such talk wasn't in his repertoire. However, even the *Colectivo* began to seem resigned to losing this particular battle, and soon their funds and energies were again channeled into campaigns against the plastic greenhouses.

So, as we moved towards winter, Ana and I resigned ourselves to the putative dam. It wasn't good for our own future, wasn't good for the valley either, but we could see that in order to stop the Rules reservoir clogging up with sludge and boulders and uprooted trees, lesser dams like ours would be needed to work as river silt traps. Deeper arguments as to whether Rules itself was a benefit – enabling the dry coastal towns to indulge in yet more tourist Gormenghasts, golf-courses and greenhouses – seemed academic in view of the fact that it was almost complete.

Besides, there were things to do. It looked as if we were going to harvest a bumper crop of olives this year and the ground beneath the trees had become a jungle of brambles and thorny pomegranate shoots. That needed clearing. There was Christmas on the way, too, with hordes of friends and family coming to stay; we would need to fix up some accommodation in the other house, which was in a state of serious dilapidation.

From time to time to time I would catch Ana looking a little pensive or preoccupied as she gazed out over the familiar view of the rivers and the gorge, but as we busied ourselves with these tasks, the threat slipped ever further from our minds.

COMFORT AND JOY

OR THE FIRST TIME SINCE we had moved to Spain, Ana and I had money for a proper Christmas bash. A royalty cheque from the book had arrived and we were pretty dazzled by it. In the past we'd had good times, but we had owed much to the generosity of our families, friends and neighbours, who would come tottering across the bridge over the festive season, bearing bags stuffed with sweets and hams and wines, and little surprises for Chloë. We would reciprocate as much as we could, of course, but there are only so many clove-and-orange pomanders that an average sock-drawer can hold, while esparto-grass bottle-coolers and preserved lemons are not the sort of presents to repeat each year. But this time we could foot the bill ourselves, buy Chloë treats and welcome our friends with all the hospitality we wished. It felt quite a privilege.

Inevitably, perhaps, as we wallowed in a new-found luxury, Ana and I would find ourselves mulling over less salubrious Christmases we'd endured in the past. Perhaps we needed to remind ourselves that life hadn't always been sunshine and lemons. Whatever, there was one Christmas that we both kept returning to: it was just after Chloë turned three and, as festivities go, it really was a washout.

That year had been exceptionally dry. The summer had burned itself out much later than usual, leaving the countryside limp and desiccated. Each day, we would stare up at the blue bowl of the sky, pinning our hopes to every wisp of haze or tiny cloud that ventured along, only to watch it disappear without trace. And then at last the weather broke. We sighed with relief as the rain started, and even went to stand in the wet, holding up Chloë, so that she could marvel at the tiny droplets that fell around her and beaded our hair.

The whole valley seemed to exude a new scent of wet dust and pines, while trees that had become pale and shrivelled turned green and then greener still as the rain washed the dust from their leaves. The trickle of the rivers soon rose to a respectable roaring and even the birds seemed pleased and flapped about the place chirping and trilling happily as if they'd won an audition to do so.

But it kept on raining and gradually the whole Alpujarras turned to porridge. Clouds and mists shrouded the valley and all the landmarks we knew disappeared. The bridge was among them, swept away downriver and cutting us off from any chance of visitors. For days we couldn't even see the mountains around us – we seemed to be alone on a misty bog of an island.

To make matters worse, Christmas loomed on the horizon. 'There's only ten days to go,' said Ana, one morning. 'Soon we'll be getting all that needle-knee music...'

'All that what?'

'Needle-knee music – you know, organ introductions to Christmas carols,' Ana explained, as if this was the only possible blot on the winter's horizon.

The ground around the house got so sodden that the water table rose and the kitchen was flooded with three inches of water. So too was Ana's end of the bedroom. We were wet and cold and bored and sniffling with colds.

Alpujarran architecture was not conceived with rain in mind and doesn't cope well with it. A frequent topic of conversation and indeed a measure of a certain sort of respectability is the quantity of buckets you have in your house collecting drips from the roof. One day I counted twenty-three receptacles dotted around the house – buckets and bowls and tins and tubs. They were worst at night; just as they filled up, one of us or one of the dogs would blunder into them, sloshing pints of muddy water over the floor. This was a regular occurrence, as the solar power system had given out and we moved like ghosts through the grey gloom or by the light of a few feeble candle-stubs. The fire, fuelled by wet black wood, filled the room with smoke and offered but a feeble and malevolent glow.

'Well, that wasn't so bad,' Bernardo told me later. 'We too had many drips from the roof. There was one right in the middle of the bed so I had to sleep with a bucket, holding it on my chest, like so' – and he mimed balancing a bucket on his ribcage – 'and every hour, I'd have to get up and go and tip it out into the bath.' I felt that all my efforts in the matter of drip-catching were as naught compared to Bernardo's heroic endurance.

The days drew into weeks and the dripping went on in the house and the mist and the rain went on outside. We kept Chloë dry by sleeping on or sitting in the wet bits ourselves, and we read her stories by candlelight and made pancakes, but little by little we were getting gloomier. 'It looks like it's brightening up a bit at last,' I would announce each morning as I looked through streaming windows at an unrelenting sea of cloud, but even I was beginning to lose heart.

I mused at the time that, if we had been rich, there might have been some way out of it. Perhaps we could have checked into a dry hotel. But we couldn't actually get across the bridge – in fact, we no longer had a bridge – and even if we had got across the river it was difficult to imagine a hotel welcoming us with our entourage of dogs, cats, horses, sheep and chickens. No, you couldn't buy your way out of this one. And besides, we weren't rich – at that very moment we didn't have more than a few hundred pesetas.

We weren't terminally broke. There was money somewhere in the pipeline – sheep subsidy, lamb sales, holiday cottage lets – but nothing to bail us out right then and there. I remember doing an audit of our resources. We had a tank of petrol in the car, a sack of onions, a sack of potatoes whose tendrils were making the larder an impenetrable thicket, fifty litres of olive oil in plastic drums, a month's chicken feed, and a few vegetables battling their way through on the vegetable patch. Oh – and we had a whole lot of olives and trees laden with oranges. We weren't going to go hungry, we just had no cash for Christmas.

The main problem was the lack of electricity. With not enough sun to charge our solar batteries there was nothing we could do to relieve the damp gloom – we couldn't even listen to music or story tapes in the dark. It's true that I had my guitar but I wasn't really in the mood for playing and Ana and Chloë were very definitely not in the mood for listening. A Christmas day around a blazing fire would be something to look forward to, but sitting in Wellington boots on the wooden chairs (the foam rubber sofa had become a sponge), choking on the smoke from the sodden hearth, fell rather short of the mark.

'Don't worry,' I said. 'Something will turn up.' Ana gave me one of the most withering looks I can recall and even Chloë looked just a shade unconvinced.

One good thing was that we weren't completely cut off. We had rigged up what we called the 'Flying Fox' – a rope and pulley – to get across the river, so we made the occasional foray to town. A few days before Christmas I swung over and walked into town to gather a few cheap provisions and check the post office box.

There was a scattering of letters and cards from family and friends and a thin airmail letter from Florida, with the name of an American friend of my mother's on the back. I had always called her an aunt but I don't think there was any actual kinship involved and I had last met her when I was at school. As I opened it, something green fluttered onto the street. It was a hundred-dollar bill. Aunt Dawn had heard that we were struggling to make ends meet and hoped the money might come in use.

When I had recovered myself, I dashed off one of Orgiva's finest Christmas cards to Aunt Dawn, and – savouring one of life's great moments – pondered how to spend the windfall. The obvious answer was a battery charger, a big powerful one that we could hook up to our generator. We would enjoy Christmas with needle-knee music and electric light – what unimaginable gaiety! I had seen a battery charger in Granada that looked just right and I figured the hundred dollars might just cover it.

The next day was Christmas Eve and just before dawn I set off in the barrelling rain on my excursion to Granada. I had left our ancient Land Rover, Black Bess, in what looked like a safe spot on the back route out, about an hour and a half's walk above the house. I trudged up the mountain with an umbrella and a backpack, round and round the bends as the rain sheeted on down.

Arriving at the car I was so saturated with water that with each step gouts of water spurted from my boots. There was nothing dry enough even to wipe my glasses on. But Black Bess rattled into action and as we moved off up through the pines the rain stopped and the impenetrable mass of cloud lifted, parted and thinned. An hour later, as I pulled into Mecina Fondales to see if I could borrow some dry clothes from a friend, the sun had burnt through the skies and the world was humming and steaming in its yellow warmth.

In Granada, the sky reformed and called in reinforcements to bathe the city in torrents. However, I was in good spirits and, armed with my windfall, I strode in and bought the battery charger. Only 12,000 pesetas! I couldn't believe my luck. There would be enough left over to buy something special to eat, and perhaps a silver ball to hang from the festive frond of Aleppo Pine that stood dripping in the corner of the lounge.

I went to a shop and bought a couple of bottles of good red wine, some chocolate tree-decorations and two pheasants. You don't see many pheasants round here so they were a special treat. In fact, we hadn't had a pheasant since our days in a tied cottage by a dual carriageway in the South of England. There Ana had had an admirer who was a gamekeeper, and sometimes as a token of his hopeless love he would festoon the porch with slaughtered gamebirds. Coming home in the dark, our faces would be flapped by pheasants hanging in the lilac trees by the gate. We feasted on them till we could face them no more.

From Granada, Black Bess and I sloshed back through the rain to the Alpujarras. The pathetic little wedges of windscreen cleaned by the wipers were woefully inadequate to see by, and the heater soon gave up its battle against the mist-shrouded windows. The rattle of the car and the hiss of the rubber on the road and the roaring of the useless heater and the rain drumming on the roof contrived to turn me into a quaking wreck by the time I reached the holm-oak. This tree marked the spot where the track was no longer safe, and I pulled in, switched the engine off, and shut my eyes in the black silence. I thought of Chloë and Ana in our dismal home deep in the valley below me. And then, unable to help myself, I fell asleep.

When I awoke all was quiet, the rain had stopped battering the roof, and half a moon and Venus sailed together amongst the fast scudding clouds. The battery charger was huge and heavy. By sailor-like art I lashed it to the outside of my backpack and heaved it up on to my back. Then I slung the pheasants over my shoulder and set off on the long haul down the hill. I started off bouncing but in minutes I was creeping. The slightest jar or jog in a step would crash the sharp steel cover of the charger into the back of my hip. It took an hour and a half to descend the track, rough at the best of times and worse than I had ever seen it, with great ruts cut by the rain, and scattered landslide boulders.

The pheasants flapped in resignation and the charger rubbed me raw, but it was a beautiful night. As I came over the brow of the hill I stopped in awe at the sight of the deep black valley and far below the two rivers raging like molten silver out through the gorge at El Granadino and down past the *vega* of Tíjolas to the Seven-Eye Bridge. I squatted by a rock to relieve my shoulders of the burning weight and held my breath to hear the silence and the distant sound of waters. Suddenly there was the sound of a huge creature galloping past. I stood up, startled, in an agonisingly awkward jerk, and looked around to see the rump of a wild boar disappearing into the brush. It had been right beside me and I could almost feel the heat of its breath.

An hour more of careful downhill creeping and I whistled to get the dogs barking. They raced up the hill to greet me, wagging their tails with simple delight. We reached the house together and I strung the pheasants up by the neck on the porch – that's what you do with pheasants – and put the charger in the shed ready to connect up on Christmas Day. Then Ana, Chloë and I spent a quiet Christmas Eve evening,

sitting erect on wooden chairs in our Wellingtons, opening cards and reading out bits of letters, and guzzling the
chocolate decorations that didn't fit on the pine branch.

We awoke late next morning and – oh, Christmas miracle –
the sun shone down from a clear morning sky, illuminating
the folds of the Contraviesa in shades of green and gold. I
was excited about giving Chloë her present even though it
was only a home-made doll's bed that I'd knocked together.
I had made it of white wood and painted a tasteful floral
motif on the headboard, while Ana had made matching
sheets and blankets and pillows. Chloë was thrilled with it
– especially as we had somehow kept the sheets and blankets dry – and with the traditional stocking presents that
Ana had wrapped for her, consisting of a mandarin or two,
some almonds, some figs, some sweets and a piece of coal
wrapped in silver paper. It's a simple truth but you don't
need to spend a lot of money to make children happy. The
spirit of Christmas had arrived, and with the feast ahead,
the wine and the battery charger, I felt full of festivity.

I threw open the door to let the sunshine in – and there
on the porch, twirling on thin strings, were the heads of
the pheasants. I had remembered hanging whole pheasants there the night before... perhaps they had rotted at the
neck and fallen. No, there was nothing on the ground. The
ghastly realisation dawned upon me. The dogs had eaten
the bodies, feathers and all, leaving us with just the heads
twirling on the porch.

I had wanted the pheasants to be a surprise for Ana
and had said nothing the night before. She saw me star-

ing open-mouthed through the door, and came over and put her arm round me. 'Oh, Chris, how lovely, you bought pheasants for our Christmas lunch...'

'Yes... but... now there's only the... the...' I couldn't bring myself to say the word.

'Heads – you mean heads, don't you? I suppose you bought whole pheasants and hung them up here where the dogs could get them.'

'Yes...' I whispered

'Never mind. It's the thought that counts and it was a really lovely thought. Anyway we can always make a soup from the heads – with some fried potatoes and eggs it'll do well enough for a Christmas dinner.'

Miserably, I trudged off to connect the battery charger up to our power system. It didn't work at all, not a spark. There was some fundamental malfunction, or else I had been sold a dud.

Still, at least the dogs hadn't drunk the wine. Ana decorated the dogs with bits of tinsel, we had fried eggs and potatoes for lunch, and we all went and sat by the river in the sunshine. I've spent worse Christmas days.

A NIGHT UP THE MOUNTAIN

J UST BENEATH THE PEAK OF MULHACÉN, which at 3450m
is the highest peak in the Sierra Nevada, indeed in the
whole Iberian peninsula, are the *borreguiles*. In days
gone by, a lamb was not considered fit to be eaten
until it had passed a summer grazing on the sweet grasses
that cloak these high mountain meadows – hence the name,
from *borrego*, which means a lamb.

There are a dozen or so *borreguiles* below the southwest
side of the peak. Each one is a great bowl of a watermea-
dow, enclosed by rock walls and communicating by water-
falls to the meadows below and above. They differ in the
arrangement of the various elements. Some have a waterfall
dropping straight into a lagoon and then two or three rills
of water meandering through the grass to the lip, where
they cascade over the edge to the meadow below. Another
may have its lagoon in the centre, and a single torrent of

water feeding it and draining it, and there's one that has a steep bank of grass for its waterfall.

Common to them all is the perfect peace, the almost supernatural clarity of the water and the springiness of the deep green grass. By August, though, even up here the vegetation starts to wither as the high mountain waters dry out. The shrivelling and crisping starts on the perimeter and creeps towards the centre, until there is just a thin stain of green around the lagoon – and then nothing, as even the water of the lagoon is sucked into the air by the summer sun, leaving a dry bed of stones. Then with the autumn rains, the *borreguiles* green up again, just in time to be buried beneath a couple of metres of snow until the following summer.

The time to see the *borreguiles* is late May to late July – that's spring in the high sierra – and somehow, the very fleeting nature of this beauty makes it all the more appealing. In early July, almost a year after our dam fiesta, I walked up to the meadows from the village of Capileira. As I clambered up over the lip, I was struck dumb by what I saw. The grass was no longer green, it was a sheet of livid blue – a blue so dazzling it seemed to come from outside the normal spectrum of perception. These were the Sierra Nevada gentians. I had heard about them but this was the first time I had ever seen them. There were two varieties in bloom – the ultramarine *Gentiana verna*, and the delicate, almost luminescent *Gentiana alpina*.

There are some things so strong you just have to share them – and those gentians were strong. As I picked my way down, I wondered how I could entice Ana and Chloë up the mountain. Like the locals, they both tend to regard walking strictly as a means of getting around, and not a pleasure for its own sake. Putting across the idea of a six-hour relentlessly uphill slog would test my powers of persuasion to the limits. But a climb up here to see the magical blue haze of the gentians seemed exactly what we all needed to shake off our worries.

Chloë, as it happened, was busy; she had an overnight stay coming up with a schoolfriend in Orgiva. But Ana seemed quite taken with the idea and, with Chloë away, was even happy to consider camping out for a night. There was nothing to prevent us setting off together the next day.

For all the splendours of the flowers and mountain scenery in store, I had a nagging worry that I might have underplayed the rigours of the day ahead. 'It's not really that far,' I had assured Ana. 'And it's not as steep as all that, and anyway, when you get there it's so wonderful that you forget instantly how far and how steep it was – which, of course, it wasn't.'

Ana receives such pronouncements with an understandable suspicion, developed over some twenty-five years of knocking around with me. But I wondered if she had applied quite the right level of scepticism. Still, I really did feel it would be worth it once we were up at the meadows: for the pleasure Ana would take from spending time there, and for the pleasure I would get from her pleasure. There was also something symbolic about the whole trip, for the *borreguiles* are the source of the Poqueira, the river that waters our farm and supplies the springs from which we drink and wash and water the flowers of our patio.

We set out as soon as we had fed the dogs, cats, chickens, pigeons, horses and sheep. Porca the parrot set out with us, on Ana's shoulder, until we reached the river and she sent him wheeling off. We climbed into the car and headed off for Pampaneira, one of the high Alpujarran villages, where our walk to the *borreguiles* would begin. Within the hour we were fortifying ourselves in the square with coffee and *roscos* – dry buns which look tantalisingly like doughnuts, but aren't – and gazing up past the churchtower at the distant peak of Veleta, which was not where we were going, but was a similar distance away.

We made our way up through the cobbled alleys of the village and up the steep woodland path to the hamlet of Bubión. From there it was just a mile, still climbing hard, through the meadows to Capileira, the highest village at nearly 1300 metres above sea-level. When I reached the village plaza, wheezing like a rusty bellows, Ana was waiting for me, sitting serenely on a bench. This annoyed me a bit, as you may imagine. 'You must learn to pace yourself,' I gasped.

'This is a nice place. Why don't we spend the rest of the day here – we could do some shopping,' teased Ana. I ignored her and, slinging my pack, marched resolutely out of the village in the direction of up. We climbed on, for hours, through pinewoods and along *acequias*. The sun was burning fiercely and the shade of the trees and even the sound of the water was a blessing.

Later, we sat beneath a pine tree and drank water from the bottles in my pack – just below the boil – and ate the usual stuff that you eat on a mountain picnic – ham and *chorizo*, olives, tomatoes, bread, and then halva, dates and about three kilos of cherries to finish. Then we slept.

The picnic pine tree was the last one; after lunch we were walking above the treeline. The sun had moved well down from its zenith, and was burning our left legs, our left arms and the left side of our faces. In the far distance we could make out the Refugio del Poqueira and, just beyond the hut, the steep river valley that we would climb to get to the *borreguiles*.

'We're not going all the way up there, are we?' asked Ana.

'You've done nothing but moan since we set off this morning,' I baited her, without a shred of justification. In fact, Ana had cheerfully led the way almost all day.

There was a treat in store for us as we walked up the long steady incline towards the refuge: the thymes and *puas* of what botanists call the 'hedgehog zone' were in flower. The term is a good one, as the low-growing spiky plants do indeed look like a vast multitude of hedgehogs. The path and its borders were a mass of pink and white domes, made up of the most exquisite densely-packed little flowers. Ana had never seen the like of it, as she hadn't been this high. I'd seen the plants and had dismissed them as rather dull, but now, in all their flowering glory, they were dazzling. The air was full of butterflies, too, some as big as your hand, and whenever we came to the tiniest patch of moisture, there would be literally clouds of Small Blues. They carpeted the ground as we approached, and as we passed they would lift in their thousands into the air, creating their own infinitesimal mountain breeze.

I grinned at Ana and she smiled back, a smile of pure delight and happiness. It was already worth it, though I knew that there was still one hell of a haul to get up to the *borreguiles*, where we planned to spend the night. The Spanish have a saying: 'If you would feel like a king, take your friends to a place of beauty that you know.' It sounds better in Spanish – and it's true.

Hours later the sun had dropped behind the peak of Veleta and the valleys were full of shadows. Ana and I were trudging on in a ponderous silence, having climbed for nearly six hours and more than 5,000 feet. I was determined that we should reach the *borreguiles* by nightfall.

This final valley, where the new-born Poqueira river tumbled among the rocks and the grass, was as steep and difficult as the first hill of the morning, only now there was not much energy left in us. However, at long last we crawled up and over into the lowest of the meadows. It was almost dark and the few gentians that were in this meadow had gone to sleep, with their petals tightly wrapped against the cold of the coming night.

Ana and I slumped on a rock, warm still from the hot sunshine of the day, and there we lay until the icy cold of the night air moved us. I set about unpacking the backpack. Sleeping bags, sweaters, bottles of water – now icy cold – food, a torch, sticking plasters, moisturising cream... 'Moisturising cream! What the hell do you want with moisturising cream?'

Ana said she wasn't going anywhere without moisturiser.

'That's all very well, but I'm the poor goon who has to carry the stuff!'

'Well, if you like I'll carry it down,' she offered.

We found a soft bed for the sleeping bags and laid our aching limbs down to get what rest we could. An hour or maybe two hours later, after endless rollings over and wriggling and other attempts to get comfortable, the full moon rose over the black rocks to the east. Our little valley flooded with the cold silver light. I rolled over again and looked at Ana.

'Are you asleep?'

'No, of course not.'

We got up and peered over the rim of the meadow. Below us lay the Alpujarras, bathed in moonlight. There was a mist that swirled in the valleys like a sea of milk, and the hills like dark islands, the Isles of the Blessed, so it seemed. The scene was cloaked in deep silence, until a dog, somewhere in the vastness of the night, started to bark. The call was taken up by a dozen other distant dogs, and for a little while the valleys rang with the sound; then the silence stole back over the night.

We watched without a word, hardly breathing for fear of breaking the spell. Then Ana shivered a little.

'God, to think that we live down there, in that.'

I grunted. When you've known one another a long time, sometimes a grunt is all you need.

'It's amazing, a privilege,' she continued as we pulled our sleeping bags around us.

I grunted again and re-arranged an arm that was losing circulation across her shoulder.

The valleys of the Alpujarras were immediately beneath us, then to the south, rearing dark from the mists, lay the great mass of the Contraviesa and the Sierra de Lújar. If we raised our eyes above the coastal hills, we could see the moonlight on the distant Mediterranean.

'Chris,' Ana whispered.

I paused.

'You know they're going to go ahead and build the dam in the valley, don't you?'

'Yes,' I answered into the darkness. 'Yes, I do.'

For the first time since we'd heard the news it seemed somehow bearable. We talked into the night, liberated by saying the unsaid, and found we had drawn much the same conclusions. We wanted to stay, even if the water and silt ate away at the farm, and so did Chloë, as far as we could tell. Whatever happened we'd first try and adapt our lives around it. We had roots here now and upping and leaving wasn't the option it had once been.

Also, we felt a sort of responsibility to stay and keep an eye on what was happening to the land – not just our own farm, but the valley, and the wider canvas of the Alpujarras. We might have lost the battle over the dam but maybe we could live with that, and use what we had learnt in battles to come.

Anyway, nothing would happen for a while, we agreed. Nothing ever happens quickly in Spain.

However beautiful it is, you don't sleep too well in a sleeping bag in a mountain meadow. We rolled and wriggled and tossed and turned and shivered, and tried not to be dazzled by the moonlight, but it was only when the sun rose that we finally got to sleep. There we remained, until the sun climbed high enough to start heating up the bags.

We crawled out, blinking at the sunshine. All around us, the gentians had opened, and all the grass was hidden beneath a haze of deepest blue. The sky was clear blue, then there were the dark rocks and the deep blue carpet of the meadow with its clear lake in the middle. It seemed that we had woken up in a quite different world.

There was nothing you could say; we just gasped. It took some time to get used to the phenomenon, and then, little by little, we came back to earth, and breakfasted on cherries and springwater. All that pain, all that relentless, sweaty climbing, it had all been worthwhile, just to wake up on one morning of your life in a place like this. Ana thought so too.

As we sat enjoying the warmth of the day, we heard a rustling, a slithering of rocks, and then the unmistakable clong of a sheep bell. There was a sheep slithering down the shaly slope above the meadow. It caught sight of us and stopped, squatted and peed, looking at us blankly. It was joined by another sheep, which did exactly the same thing. Sheep always do this for some reason; when they see a person, they squat and pee – unless of course they happen to be rams, in which case they just stand around and dribble.

The pair were joined by another and another and soon there was a flock of several hundred sheep bowling down off the rocks into the meadow, bleating and bongling with dozens of bells. They spread out, filling the valley from one side to the other. They drank deep from the lake, and then set about eating the gentians. It took them about half an hour, and when they had finished there wasn't a single flower left; the meadow had returned to its green.

Ana and I were the last to see the gentians that year. We headed back down the hill wondering if there were some philosophical point we had just seen demonstrated, but unable to establish what it might have been. Perhaps it had something to do with grasping the fleeting moment before some damn herbivore comes along and grasps it first.

It took us most of a long hot day to get back down to Pampaneira and the car. We were exhausted and silent as we trudged downward, every jolt a burning pain in knee and thigh muscles. As we drove on to the valley, we noticed a plume of dust rising from the riverbed and heard what sounded like the roar of heavy machinery.

When we reached our bridge we had to wait to allow Domingo's sheep to come across. Domingo himself was on the other side, counting them as they passed.

'There's a machine in the valley,' he announced. 'Down by El Granadino. They've started on the dam.'

POND LIFE

W E SET OFF NEXT MORNING for El Granadino, to see for ourselves what the machine was up to in the riverbed. It was a still, fiercely hot day, but near the gorge there is always a breeze, and as we approached its tall red cliffs, the cool air fanned our faces. We clambered up over a heap of stones. 'Oh my God! Look at that, will you!' Ana exclaimed. A huge yellow earth-moving machine was asleep beneath the cliffs. Beside it the cliff-face was laid bare, reduced by the voracious gnawing of the machine to its skeleton. The very roots of the mountain lay picked clean, gouged out like cavities in a tooth.

We looked at the gruesome scene in silence; there wasn't much you could say. It seemed such an intrusion, such an act of wanton violence perpetrated upon the quiet valley and its untidy, boulder-strewn riverbed. This had been a place of perfect peace. We would come down here on summer evenings to enjoy the breeze and sit and watch the swallows and bats skimming and dipping to drink from the water. We walked slowly back up the river, each of us lost in our own thoughts.

When we reached the farm, we came upon Trev. He was busy hauling hosepipes about the place. It had been so long since we had done any serious concerted work on the pool that it took a while for the implication to sink in.

'Morning, Maestro,' I said, rather more breezily than I felt. 'Don't tell me you're actually going to fill this pool with water...'

'I can't think what else I'm going to do with these hoses,' he answered dryly as he wedged the end of the pipe between two rocks by the fish pond.

'Well, it'll be interesting to see if the pool fills with water before the valley fills with river-sludge,' I said darkly.

Trev looked at me closely. 'It's not like you to talk like that.'

'You can't really blame me. Ana and I have just been down looking at the work on the dam. There's not much doubt that it's going ahead now.'

'Chris, you can't seriously believe that the huge area of the valley is going to fill up in your lifetime. To reach even the stable there'd have to be a tailback halfway to Torvizcón.' Torvizcón is a village at least six kilometres upriver.

'Do you really think that? Because that's exactly what I think, only I find it hard to take my own opinions seriously.'

'Look,' said Trev, sitting down beside me. 'Just look at the size of these river valleys. I've been doing some calculations on my computer. They're meaningless, of course: nobody can come up with real figures for this kind of thing. But I reckon the volume of silt you'd need to reach the level we're sitting at now would be several billion cubic metres. The likelihood of your losing even the river fields in your lifetime is pretty remote. You really shouldn't worry, you know.'

Trev's pronouncement was nothing new. He'd been saying more or less the same for months now, as I fretted away over the dam. Yet somehow his words resonated this time – bringing with them a reassurance that took me by surprise. I grinned at Trev. 'Maybe you're right – we shouldn't worry,' I said and turned back to look at the pool. 'So we're really going to get to swim in it at last... I can hardly believe it.'

'I wouldn't get that excited if I were you...'

'Why? When will it be full?'

'Well, taking into account the elliptical shape, the progressive broadening of the steps and the angle of incline between the shallow and the deep end – and then allowing for a sluggish flow of, say, eleven litres a minute, and some evaporation – it ought to take about nine days.' Trev paused to rub his nose. 'That's providing you don't use the water for anything else.'

We looked at the trickle of water spreading across the tiled floor of the eco-sphere. The rate of flow was so feeble that it was difficult to see how it would ever reach the top.

As Manolo had pointed out at the onset, people who build swimming pools in these parts expect them to be ready for a dip within a fortnight. Not so our eco-sphere (for swimming). It had been twelve months in the making and even now it was not complete. Trev still had the waterwheel to create, though for the moment he had rigged up a much less aesthetically pleasing, and rather less efficient, pump.

As so often, both Chloë and Ana had been a little suspicious of my enthusiasm right from the start of the lunatic project. As the months dragged on, and great gaps appeared in the schedule as we awaited delivery of one or other vital part or material, they began to suggest I might be foolishly in thrall to the *Arquitecto* and his schemes. Then we got the news of the dam and – even to me – the eco-sphere pool began to seem a frivolous, and costly, distraction. There were weeks when I would skirt past the seemingly abandoned site, unwilling to confront the idea that it might all be some grand white elephant. But then Trev would reappear and we would sit, legs dangling, above the concrete hole while he explained for the hundredth time the calculations of volume and lifting-power, and the exquisite complexity of the actual form of the pool. I maintained a kind of faith in the project and took comfort from the simple beauty of the filtering pond with its fish, its rocks and reeds, its lilies and velvety black dragonflies, its water-boatmen and tadpoles, and the slender little water-snake that had decided to move in.

Every morning I would cast a furtive look to see whether or not the water-level had actually risen. It looked no different, though Trev, who would be fooling around somewhere with a level and a tape-measure or a slide-rule, assured me that it was all coming along according to his calculations. And then one morning, nine days later, there was the water, brimming over the top and slopping right over the edge, coursing down the stone runnels and cascading over the rocks into the fish pond – to the consternation of the fish. Trev was looking at it pensively, massaging the side of his nose.

'God, Trev!... It works! Look, it's full of water and it's working. It's amazing!'

'No,' said Trev. 'It's not quite right; the water is moving too fast along the runnels for the ultra-violet rays to be fully effective in the purification process. We're going to have to raise the levels a touch.'

'Oh, that seems a pity... it looks alright to me.'

'Well it isn't, but it'll do for the time being. I'm off to England tomorrow. I'll sort it out when I get back.'

'What are you going to England for?'

'I'm going on a course.'

'What sort of a course?'

'Personal development – of a kind,' said Trev with what I thought was just a touch of archness.

'When will you be back, then?'

'I'll be gone for a month at least.'

'A month! But you can't, you haven't finished the pool yet!'

'It'll be alright; it'll do you for the rest of the summer.'

'And what if it doesn't work?'

'It will work. I know it will. I've done the calculations.'

'Bloody hell, Trev, you've got a nerve, buggering off right in the middle of a job!'

'Look, apart from anything else, it'll be a lot nicer for you lot if you can have the pool to yourselves for the rest of the summer, without me hanging around the place all the time.

Also I've got to go tomorrow or I'll be late for the course, and I don't want to miss out on this one...'

'Okay. So what course is it then?'

Trev looked fixedly at the bubble in his level.

'Tantric Sex, residential,' he said.

'Aah... I see,' I said thoughtfully. 'No, you don't want to be late for that.'

So Trev left to disport himself in Yorkshire, leaving us free to fool around in the crystal clear water of our new swimming-hole.

'Look,' I said to Ana. 'You can even see the bottom!'

'Hmm,' she said. 'So you can.'

But the next day the bottom had disappeared altogether.

'You can't see the bottom at all now,' Chloë observed.

'Yes, I know, but that's only natural, and besides, I think a green tinge makes the water look even more inviting, don't you?'

Chloë and Ana were unsure about this. And the next day a number of the lower steps had gone the way of the bottom.

'I think it gives it something of the look of a woodland pool, which is rather nice,' I suggested in response to the criticism.

But over the next few days the woodland pool became a thin miso soup, which thickened and greened up at an alarming rate. By the end of the week it had become an opaque sludge of mephitic green with a layer of slime floating on the surface. I was the only one left swimming.

'Oh come on, Chris, you can't – it's disgusting.'

'I admit, it doesn't look terribly appetising, but unless I'm mistaken I think it's just the tiniest bit cleaner today – you can almost make out the second step.'

All week I had been trying hard to remain positive. The slime seemed to mean the failure of the whole system, although as far as I could tell all the various elements were functioning properly. There was sunshine all through each long day to power the electric pumps, so the water was being lifted perfectly well into the sand-filter. Thence it was seeping at a proper rate through the sand back into the bottom of the pool, where it set up its circulatory current. Then it spilled over the top, where the sun was impregnating with its ultra-violet rays the sheets of water that coursed thinly down the stone channels. From there it poured into the fish pond where the fish eagerly glooped up the algae and other organisms inimical to the clarity of our water. All this seemed to be working... so what was going wrong?

A little knot of spleen was starting to form somewhere inside me. This whole swimming-pool scheme was a balls-up, a failure; I had been gulled, taken for a mug. Here were my family and me standing disconsolately on the edge of an evil-looking basin of water, that even the rankest hippo-potamus would hesitate to wallow in, while the architect of this foul scheme was off in the north of England, cavorting with the *houris* of Hull. It was all too galling. I felt suddenly ashamed that I had put so much faith into his prognosis about the dam. Clearly the man hadn't a clue.

I decided to phone Trev and have it out with him there and then.

'What do you mean by "that's supposed to happen"?' I found myself spluttering, almost as soon as he answered the phone.

'I mean just that. That the water goes through this stage...'

'Look, Trev, I'm not an unreasonable man, but I really don't think it's too much to ask that...'

'Just calm down and listen...' he insisted. I didn't expect him to be so unruffled and it rather took the wind from my sails. 'It's all part of the scheme of things, you see. You have to get through the muck stage for the water to go clear. I knew this was going to happen. Don't, whatever you do, change the water or you'll have to start all over again, but watch closely and you'll see it clearing. It'll take about a week.'

'Oh... alright. How's the course coming on, then?'

A week after I put the phone down, the bottom reappeared. You could just make out the lines of the tiles, and not long after, the water regained its original clarity. The fish were fat as balls and the filaments were filthy, but the water of the eco-sphere was clear as air – well, almost. I was over the moon. I even phoned Trev up to tell him that it was working as he had said. 'Told you so,' he said. I don't know what else I expected really.

The pumps hummed quietly to themselves and the solar tracker tracked the sun; the sun's rays poured down on the stones, slaughtering enemy bacteria by the million. The fish in the filter pond ate anything that erred into their orbit. They were carp, which we learned later are the goats of the fish world and were no good for our eco-system. Carp eat everything – tadpoles, froglets, water-boatmen, dragonflies – they'd eat people if they could.

We had bought five more little carp to keep the original two big ones company, reassured by the man in the fish shop, who said they'd be fine, as fish absolutely never eat their own species. But within a day they had all been wolfed down by the big carp. Don't be fooled; carp are bad news.

There was something else that we hadn't put in the calculations about our eco-sphere – something we should, perhaps, have thought of right from the start. The pool was a paradise for frogs. To an extent we had ourselves to blame, as we'd helped Chloë introduce a bucket of tadpoles from the riverbed, thinking it would be good to have a frog or two about the place. But whatever nutrients existed in the pond, they were just what frogs like best, and before long the population had reached critical mass and was forced to send out scouts in search of new waters to colonise. Those that went southwest had a long journey before they reached the river, and the river is a very unreliable environment for frogs anyway; but those that headed northeast soon came back with the news that not four good hops away was a glorious expanse of limpid water, ripe for the taking.

Now I don't mind swimming in a pool with a dozen frogs or so in there with me – you barely see them – and even twenty frogs would not be unacceptable, though I'm perhaps in the minority here. It wasn't long, however, before I began to worry that our pool would become a heaving mass of frogs, croaking and copulating. It was a ghastly thought but what could we do? Using some sort of chemical for their discouragement was out of the question because the whole point of the pool was that it should be chemical-free and ecological – well, it certainly was that! Also a chemical deterrent for frogs was unlikely to be beneficial to bathers. So instead, I was forced to devote many hours each day to taking out the frogs and tadpoles.

Of course frog-hunting has its element of fun, and is a very skilled business. Frogs are fast movers and don't like to be scooped up in a net, and, in our case, returned to a grubby old side-pond. And when I did catch them and return them to their own part of the pool, it didn't take them long to turn round and hop straight back.

We needed some advice, but when I mentioned my concern on the telephone to Trev, he sighed in resignation as if I were some sort of half-wit. 'You can't seriously be bothered by a few frogs in the water! Look how beautiful they are, how gracefully they swim. I mean for heaven's sake, man, it's not the Ritz, is it?' Then he went on to reassure me that the carp could more than manage to keep the population in order.

Chloë, needless to say, was thrilled with the swimming pool. It was a delight to see her spend long summer days playing in the water with her friends, running in and out of the foliage before diving in with the frogs. A shriek of laughter usually meant that Porca had arrived to take up his customary swimming perch on top of Ana's head, where he would remain while Ana glided carefully up and down.

Not long after the pool was filled I lay floating on the water and looking out across the valley. Ana swam cautiously across to me with Porca. Below us the river snaked calmly along at a rate that would take a millennium to bury our home under its silt.

'You know,' I said to Ana. 'I think Trev may have got it right, after all.'

'Well, it will be better when we get the waterwheel up and running,' she answered.

'No, I meant what he said about the dam and the water-levels in the riverbed. I really believe he's right, you know, and the farm's going to be okay – and the valley, too.'

Ana shrugged. 'Time will tell,' she said, and ducked slowly beneath the water, leaving Porca to jump ship with a loud squawk and a flurry of wingbeats.

From deep in the jungle of the pond the frogs opened their throats and croaked a great croak into the warm evening air.

And then what happened?

CHRIS STEWART BRINGS EVENTS UP TO DATE

Ten years on from the publication of Driving Over Lemons, **Chris Stewart** talks about life at El Valero, what's changed in his valley, how the success of the books has affected him and his neighbours, and whether he ever regrets leaving Genesis.

Chris, the first thing everyone always wants to know is – are you still living on the farm, at El Valero?

It's funny how often people ask that. They tend to say: 'Are you still living on that dump of a farm you describe in the books, or have you moved to some marble-clad villa in Marbella?'

Clearly those people have not read the books! Either that or I have failed absolutely to get the

message across. The answer is a crystal-clear yes. After twenty years, we still greatly enjoy living here, and the only way we are leaving is in a box – and not even then, as a matter of fact, as both Ana and I would like to be buried beneath an orange tree on the farm.

Mind you, I do sometimes wonder if we could have stayed at El Valero without the books and the royalties we earn from them. A lot of farmers, and especially organic farmers, find they simply can't get by without some other source of income. It was pretty fortunate that our source turned out to be writing books.

Do you still feel the same way about the farm as when you moved here?

I had just turned forty when we bought El Valero; Ana was a few years younger. Looking back, it was a good age for a move. We could manage the constant round of work and still have energy left to look about us and make improvements. I can't imagine starting out on some of those schemes today – fencing off the hillside for the sheep, for example, was an absolute killer of a task.

Curiously, during the first years I grew convinced that the one thing we needed to put everything in order was a tractor – as if it was a universal panacea that would sweep away the drudgery of farm work. I remember thinking, when I was offered a contract for Driving Over Lemons, 'Maybe, I'll be able to buy that tractor.'

And when I got my first royalty cheque, I did buy a tractor – a ropey old model which had reached the end of its useful life in Sussex. It was a vehicle that should have been put out to rust rather than shipped to Spain, especially to a farm like ours. I drove it for a few weeks but found it completely terrifying, wobbling and tipping on the tiniest of inclines. Which is the way a hell of a lot of farmers go, with a tractor tipping on top of them. So I've kept a pretty wide berth from it ever since.

Did the success of *Driving Over Lemons* have any immediate impact, beyond buying tractors?

It gave us freedom from daily worries about money – that's a very welcome thing. It was a relief to no longer be pitied by friends or family, who thought

we had been daft to sink all our money into a subsistence farm. And I no longer had to tear myself away from the farm to go shearing in the gloom of the Swedish winter, or do the rounds so much in Andalucía. Not that I regret all those shearing expeditions in the high mountains. They gave me an insight into a vanishing way of life, a ready source of stories, and a lot of local friends. We would have had a very different experience of Spain if we hadn't needed to go out and find paid work.

The book also carried some sense of vindication of the crazy decision we had taken when we upped sticks and moved here. Even my mother, who had always hoped I would live in a nice Queen Anne house in the south of England, volunteered that she now almost understood what it was that we saw in the place.

Just how tough was it in the early days?

I'm not sure we stopped to think about it. We weren't exactly hand-to-mouth, as the shearing brought in enough for us to get by on, given that we had the fruits of the farm. We always

Driving over the river, with Chloë aged about five. The farm really is on the wrong side of the river – and we still have to ford it to get across.

had fresh orange juice, olives, wonderful vegetables, and an occasional leg of lamb. But we were, I suppose, pretty close to the breadline, which I think did us good. It would be foolish to extol the virtues of poverty, but you can learn a lot from a few years of straitened circumstances. For us, it bound us as a family and rooted us on the farm. We had to make things work because that was how we fed ourselves.

Were you prepared for the book's success?

Every publisher makes it their first task to tell an author, once they have commissioned their book, that they won't make a bean out of it. And mine were the same: 'Don't give up the day job,' they said. Not that there was any choice about that. If you're a farmer, you can't. I had no inkling that my whole life was going to turn around and the writing would become the thing that I do.

Although your books are sold as 'Travel', you actually stay at home!

That's right. I hardly move from the farm from one chapter to the next in Driving Over Lemons, though the orbit extends to Seville and back to Britain in A Parrot in the Pepper Tree, and there's a chapter in Morocco in the third book, The Almond Blossom Appreciation Society.

But the main things I write about are the kind of everyday things that happen to all of us, in our different ways. Children growing up and leaving home to become students, as has just happened to us with Chloë. And all the peculiarities of life – the snarl-ups and delights – which are perhaps odder for us because of the remoteness of where we live.

Of course, in Spain, where I have recently been published, they really can't put my books under travel, so they put them under 'Self-Help', along with books on the spiritual path and harvesting your inner energy. Strange bedfellows.

You've become a bestseller in Spain over the past couple of years. Have your neighbours now read the books?

When Driving Over Lemons was published, Domingo – my nearest neighbour and the book's true hero – got his partner Antonia to translate and read it to him... but only the bits in which he appeared. Later, when it came out in Spanish, he read a chapter every night before going to sleep. Of course, he never mentioned this to me, though he told Antonia that he enjoyed the book.

But the funny thing about Domingo is that he is not Domingo at all – he has a quite different name. For many months, as I was writing the book, I would tell him that I was writing a book in which he appeared as a major character. Would it be okay to use his name or would he rather I change it? 'Me da igual,' he would say in his typically Alpujarran way; 'It's all the same to me.' I was pleased because I felt I had created an affectionate portrait of a good friend, and it felt right to use his real name.

Well, I asked him again and again, just to make sure, and each time received the same assurance. And then, at the last possible moment, he came up to the house, very animated, and said: 'Cristóbal, I've been talking to somebody who knows about these things and he tells me that I could get into a lot of trouble as a result of this book – legal problems and family problems and God knows what else. So I want my name changed.'

I could see that somebody in a bar had been spreading a bit of mala leche –'bad milk'– as the

Lemons and Parrots in Spanish

Spanish put it. I was a bit sorry about it, but he was adamant, so I set about changing the names of all his relatives and his farm, and so on. Of course, anybody local reading the book would still know exactly who Domingo was, but he didn't seem to mind that. As far as he was concerned, as long as the character was called a different name, it wasn't officially him.

Then, as time marched on, my-friend-aka-Domingo, inspired and encouraged by Antonia (who, of course, isn't called Antonia), took up sculpture and started making a bit of a name for himself by creating the most

dazzling bronze figures of animals. By this time Lemons was selling like hot buns. And so he decided to go for an alias – and to my great delight chose to call himself, for artistic purposes, Domingo.

What about your other neighbours? What was the reaction like from them?

There was a bit of everything. One woman in Orgiva complained very publicly that I had not painted an accurate picture of the people of the town, 'because we don't eat chickens' heads'. Apparently *everything else was fine: it was just the culinary stuff that stuck in her throat, so to speak. Well, having comprehensively researched the subject of chicken head cuisine, I can say authoritatively that some Orgiveños do and some of them don't. I know this because I've had the pleasure of sharing the odd chicken's head myself.*

The locals in general began to register the success of the book because people started to turn up clutching copies. This gave a bit of a boost to the drooping Orgiva economy, which made me popular with the café owners. Antonio Galindo, who owns the bakery, a café, two bars and a discoteca, embraced me publicly in the high street and said I had turned his fortunes around. So that felt good. And not long after, I was honoured to be the recipient of the Manzanilla Prize for Services to 'Convivencia y Turismo' (which loosely translates as 'harmony between cultures and tourism'). This singular honour was manifested in the form of a tin sculpture of a manzanilla (camomile) plant – what the Spanish often call a pongo (as in the phrase 'Dónde demonios lo pongo?', which means 'Where the devil do I put this?').

News of the award got into the national paper, El Pais, where it was seen by an anthropology professor, who then published a scathing letter stating that I had contributed more to the dilution and demise of Spanish culture than any other single person. That shook me a bit, and a few days later I was stopped on the road into town by Rafael, who farms olives, oranges and vegetables in Tijola, our nearest village. 'I have just read your book, Cristóbal,' he boomed. I hung my head to await the worst. 'You are the greatest writer of the Alpujarra,' he intoned. 'You are...', he paused searching for a very particular epithet, 'a Rambo of the mind'.

It's the nicest critical review I've ever had.

So is it the people, as much as the farm, that keep you in Andalucía?

Without a doubt. We've been made incredibly welcome here. And the Spanish rural way of life suits us. But the land has got into our blood, too. When you spend twenty-odd years building and gardening and planting trees on a plot of land, you develop a connection that runs deeper than the normal sense of 'home'. All those repetitive chores of tilling, sowing and harvesting exert a subtle influence that affects the essence of who you are. And if you believe that you are what you eat, then we've become Andaluz through and through, since for two decades now we have turned the earth and pulled up vegetables, picked fruit from the trees on the terraces we've tended, collected and eaten the eggs from the chickens whose care is the first imperative of every day, and eaten the sheep that graze amongst the wild plants that grow on the hills around the house.

And there's the water, too. Nearly eighty percent of us, give or take a few bottles of wine, is made up from the water from our very own spring – I've wondered a little what we look like inside, given the amount of limescale at the bottom of our kettle. But I feel sure this place has seeped into us. We've been formed by all the little griefs and agonies, and triumphs and delights, that have peppered our lives since we moved here.

So how could you ever leave a place like this? How could you sell it? How could you put up with estate agents tramping around it with notebooks and snooty clients pointing out loudly how sub-standard and ill-conceived everything is? El Valero was never a buying and selling property. We didn't buy it as an investment; we bought it as a home. Which is lucky because it may well be the only property in Spain worth less than it cost twenty years before... and I'm glad because I've never wanted to sell the place anyway.

What do you think Spaniards in general see in the books? You'd think the humour is peculiarly English.

I thought so, too, and the books weren't published here for some years. But it turns out that the Spaniards find just the same bits funny as the British. They enjoy the way the rural Spanish are portrayed. I've had all sorts of people coming up, some of whom I didn't know could even read, wanting to tell me the bits they find funny. That said, the urban Spaniards think that we are completely bonkers. Our farm – and the Alpujarras – is very far from the spotless way that most modern Spaniards like to live.

Translation's a funny thing, though. I was interviewed by two young Taiwanese journalists, who explained to me what a humorous book the Chinese had found Driving Over Lemons. Out of curiosity I asked them if they could translate the title. I know a bit of Chinese and it struck me as peculiarly long. They scratched their heads, then said Sheep's Cheese and Guitar Heaven: a Ridiculous Drama of Andalucia.

What did Chloë think about the books?

Well, she was mystified by the English title! I have a vivid memory of her worried face when she first heard us discussing it. 'Driving Over Lemons – an Octopus In Andalucía... what on earth does that mean?' I think she was about seven at the time. So ever since then I have been the 'Octopus in Andalucía'.

She once said she would much rather I wrote novels: to her, my books are really just diary pieces and too familiar to be interesting. But secretly I think she gets quite a kick out of my success. A few months ago, she went to open a bank account in Granada, and as she handed across her ID card, the woman behind the counter exclaimed, 'Ay, Chloë Stewart... you must be the girl in the book! Ay, how I

loved the book.' It's no bad thing to be known at the bank.

Do you think Chlöe – or Ana – might write her own version of life at El Valero one day?

No. Ana has not the remotest desire to write, although she types with style and wit. (And has just reminded me that she might still go into competition with a plot for a 'body-stripper book'). It's hard to say with Chloë; I hope that we've given her a childhood that could give her something to write about. But right now she's a university student – and has flown the nest. She shares a flat in Granada and, as you might expect, has euphorically embraced urban life. Nothing is more likely to induce an enthusiasm for all things urban than a country childhood.

So now there's just Ana and me again on the farm, rattling like peas in a drum. This has been a tough rite of passage, and nobody tells you about it. You spend eighteen years living your life around, and for, your offspring in the most unimaginably close and intimate way... and then they're gone. There's nobody to wake in the morning and make sandwiches and breakfast for before heading off to the school bus.

Of course, we get a lot of pleasure from Chloë's happiness in her new life, and we're proud of her independence and her making her way in the world. But it's an odd stage, nonetheless.

What is the menagerie cast these days? You've got the sheep, and chickens...

It's the same old crew really, with occasional losses due to 'natural wastage', which of course is where I'm headed myself. The top of the pecking order is the wife, my favourite member of the menagerie, along with Chloë – who still, I think, sees this as her home. Then there's there the unspeakable parrot, Porca, Ana's lieutenant and familiar, who arrived by chance to make his home with us about nine years ago. This creature is one of the villains of my second book, A Parrot in the Pepper Tree.

The parrot dominates the five cats, who range far and wide on the farm, feasting abundantly on rats. Then there are two dogs: Big, a hairy terrier we found abandoned by the road, and Bumble, an enormous and amiable mongrel, whose function is to monopolise the space before the fire and bark at intruders. And since we're so remote and there are few visitors, he and Big keep in practice by barking all night long at the boar and foxes and other nocturnal creatures. Which makes it hard to sleep.

The dozen or so chickens earn their keep by providing us, as you might expect, with eggs. And we've got a colony of fan-tailed doves, which are on the increase again after a winter when a pair of Bonelli's eagles reduced their number from around a hundred to just seven. They are more cautious now and don't go outside much. Paco, my pigeon-fancier friend and telephone engineer, is going to get me some stock from Busquistar, up in the high Alpujarra. Apparently those pigeons know how to deal with eagles, because the crags and valleys up there are thick with them.

And finally there's the sheep, and there always will be the sheep, for I cannot imagine the dull silence of the farm without the bongling of the bells and the bleating of lambs. They provide us with the most delicious meat and, take it from me, eating home-grown lamb is one of the best treats of country life. The flock keeps the grass beneath the orange and olive trees neatly trimmed like a lush lawn. And then they range far and wide on the hills above the house, grazing on the woody aromatic plants that grow there: rosemary, thyme, broom, anthyllis, wild asparagus. At night they return to the stable, and there they copiously deposit the little heaps of beads and berries that, trodden into the straw, make the rich dung which goes to nourish the fruit and vegetables and, at one remove, us. The whole, wonderful circular ecological system.

It sounds like farming is still a passion, even if you've become more of a writer than a farmer.

I've loved farming since I discovered it at twenty-one, but if truth be told I'm not very good at it. Maybe it is a vocational gift, like medicine or music, neither of which I'm particularly good at, either. I long for the model farm, but under my care weeds seem to get the upper hand, the livestock seize every chance to destroy the plants, and every agricultural villain seems to be stalking me – mosaic virus, red spider, scale insect, aphids, blossom-end rot. You name it.

Orange trees and sheep – the mainstay of the El Valero eco-system

So it is lucky that, in terms of making a living, I've gravitated to becoming a writer. Albeit a writer who spends a lot more time farming than writing. If you've spent your life doing physical work it's hard to take entirely seriously the idea of sitting down for a day's work at a computer. I still do a bit of shearing, too, which is something I am quite good at – and which nobody else around here can do, except my-friend-aka-Domingo. So at least there's something that enables me to hold my head up in an agricultural way.

I made a living out of shearing for thirty years, but it's hard when you hit your fifties, and now I only do a few days a year – my own sheep, Domingo's, and one or two other jobs in the village. I dread these shearing days because I know what a physical effort it's going to be. But when I actually get down and stuck in, it's like dancing a dance you knew and loved long ago. Also, I get to see my handiwork year-round, idling on the hillsides, happily scratching themselves.

And it means that people still know me around the town as the Englishman who shears sheep. I know most of the farmers and they'll come and holler into my ear in bars. So I've got two different kinds of local identities. The sheep man and the book man.

You originally had a peasant farm with no running water, no electricity, no phone for miles around. Are things now very different?

We still rely on solar power, but more and better – enough, in fact, to run a freezer, which is a boon. Meantime, our house becomes ever more ecological. We've just installed 'green roofs' – a flat roof, lined and covered with soil and drought-resistant plants and grasses – by means of which insulation we have managed to raise the winter temperature in our bedroom to a comfortable six degrees. And we've got a solar water heating system that I'm currently working on.

If it weren't for the great thug of a four-wheel drive parked on the track, our carbon footprint would be virtually nothing at all. That has become of the utmost importance to us... and, at the risk of sounding sanctimonious, so it should be to all of us.

You care a great deal about environmental issues. Do you think your views have become more trenchant since moving to Spain?

I'm not so sure about that. I was a pretty trenchant ecologist long before I moved to Spain. But one of the amazing things about writing a successful book is that people suddenly start to listen to what you have to say. This is rather gratifying, as you may imagine, but it's not that you are saying anything different. It's just that you no longer have to raise your voice to be heard. I think it's the duty of anybody who finds themselves with access to the public ear to use that platform to expound ideas for reducing the sum total of human damage and misery.

The building of a dam casts a shadow over both Driving Over Lemons and its sequel, A Parrot in the Pepper Tree. How did that work out?

Well, as you can see, we're not underwater yet. By great good

Up the mast during an epic trip across the Atlantic, told in Chris's new book, Three Ways to Capsize a Boat

luck, the authorities ended up building a dam much lower than their original plan, so unless they knock it down and start again the water level will never affect our farm. It is a sediment trap rather than a reservoir, so it's filling up at a great rate with rich alluvial silt, which is wonderful for spreading on the land. It's beautiful, too, the way the river meanders amongst the banks of mud, and there's an aquatic ecosystem developing there, with ducks and herons and legions of frogs.

Talking of water, in your latest book, *Three Ways to Capsize a Boat*, you leave the land altogether to recall some epic and extremely funny seafaring adventures.

I'm glad you enjoyed it. Yes, Capsize is a book that I had to get out of my system. It seems odd, but I found myself writing snippets of it throughout the last ten years, maybe even longer. It was as if my mind was fixating on the sea. In buying El Valero I had to make a choice between the mountains and the coast. It's curious how being born and raised in inland Sussex I should come to see these two types of landscape – neither of them prominent around Horsham – as somehow fundamental to my wellbeing.

I chose the mountains, and have lived in them very contentedly for twenty years, but I do have a yearning for the sea, which comes from my early thirties when I had a brief life-changing encounter. It all started when I talked my way into a job skippering a yacht in Greece – without knowing how

to sail. So I had to learn, and one thing led to another and I ended up crewing across the North Atlantic. It marked me for life. Writing about it was fun. I didn't have any notes, because back in those days I didn't have the remotest intention of becoming a writer, but many of the experiences I had were so vivid that they all came flooding back. It was a great pleasure, too, thinking myself back to the sea, reliving it in a sense.

The trouble is that it has opened that old wound, and I am now to be found at any hour of the day or night lost in a reverie, staring at pictures of wooden sailing boats and wondering if I ever might own one.

My plan, a new gauntlet that I am throwing down for myself, is to sail around the world before I finally slip away. Not with all the ballyhoo and fol de rol of round-the-world racing and record-breaking. I'm not that sort. For me it's a matter of ambling slowly around it and wondering at all the terrible, immeasurable beauty of it. Ana indulges these crazed notions with diplomacy and tolerance. I have suggested that she may be permitted a pot of basil on the stern rail in lieu of a farm and garden – and, I suppose, having the beastly parrot along would be most appropriate.

It sounds like you were pretty smitten with the Greek islands, too. You enthusiastically describe sailing to Spetses, before embarking on your Atlantic adventures.

There's a whole lot to be said for Greece: it has the mountains and the sea in the most glorious combination, as well as the gorgeous influence of Byzantium and the Levant. And its great advantage over Spain is that the Greeks have so far not destroyed the beauty of their coasts and islands. If they do, the old gods will never forgive them.

I could have happily lived in Greece, with its sea and mountains, and the olives and oranges and the Mediterranean climate to go with it. But I always had a romance about Spain, its language, music and culture, and the great cities of Sevilla, Granada and Córdoba. So I have no terrible regrets.

One final question that you are always being asked is your role in Genesis. You were in the

Even the Spanish seem obsessed with Genesis – and my schoolboy career as their drummer. I'm on the right here, pouting next to Peter Gabriel.

original band. Can you tell us more about this?

I wrote about this a bit in A Parrot in the Pepper Tree, where I confess that I was never a very good drummer. The other members of the band very sensibly threw me out when I was just seventeen, having played on just two not very good songs on the first album. So I narrowly missed rock stardom. Actually, with me on board I fear that they would have got nowhere – and, once Phil Collins took my place, they did rather well for themselves, for which I'm delighted.

Our paths cross from time to time, and I'm always surprised by how they've managed to surf the vicissitudes of celebrity life and come through unscathed. I get the vaguest sense of it even here in Spain, where Genesis have a huge following. I emerged one day from an interview in a recording studio in Madrid to find no fewer than four young recording engineers lined up to shake the hand of a founder member of the great band.

If you could do it all over again, would you still have thrust a wad of notes into Pedro's hands and bought El Valero?

Without a moment's hesitation. And, if I'd known things were going to turn out the way they did, I'd have given him double the asking price. If I'd had the money, of course, which I didn't. I don't think there's anything better you can do in the middle of your life than to pick it up and shake it around a bit. Do something different, live somewhere different, talk another language. All that keeps your destiny on the move and keeps your brain from becoming addled. So there you have it – maybe the Spanish are right and Driving Over Lemons really is a self-help book.